W9-ANG-039

ORPHEUS

Also by Ann Wroe

Lives, Lies and the Iran-Contra Affair
A Fool and his Money: Life in a Partitioned Medieval Town
Pilate: The Biography of an Invented Man
Perkin: A Story of Deception
Being Shelley: The Poet's Search for Himself

ORPHEUS

The Song of Life

Ann Wroe

THE OVERLOOK PRESS
NEW YORK, NY

Contents

This book is dedicated to everyone who protested, 'But Orpheus isn't *real*.'

'That is the essential: to see everything *within* life itself, even the mystical, even death.'

Rilke

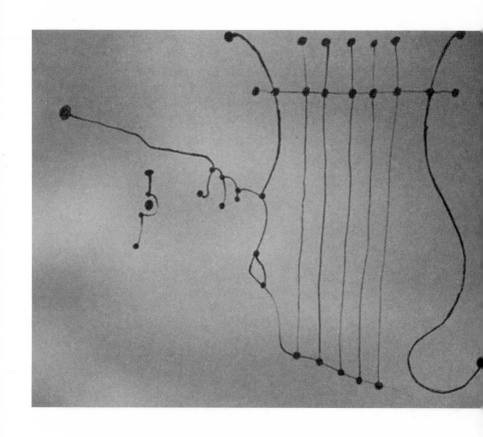

Orphée (title sequence), 1950

First string: Winter

On the morning of February 2nd 1922, Rainer Maria Rilke went up to his study and shut the door.

He was a slight man with large blue eyes that seemed, on cold days, to brim continuously with water. With a handkerchief, he dabbed the tears away. Neatness was in his nature. He wore a perfectly knotted tie; for his morning walks along empty country lanes, a homburg carefully brushed, and a cane in hand; well-shined shoes. His drooping moustache was meticulously clipped, hiding a sensual mouth above a weak, timid chin.

For his first five years his parents had named him and dressed him as a girl. They had then dispatched him to a brutal military academy. The damage was lasting. Against the odds he had become an Austrian poet of distinction, whose books by 1914 sold in thousands and went into several editions. But he retained a certain delicacy, an air of shyness, that hid his steel resolve and drew protective and passionate women into his life. One of them, Merline Klossowska, had helped him find this place to work in: a small, square fortress called the Château de Muzot, without electricity or running water, in the foothills of the French Alps.

The study looked out on the pretty woods and vineyards of the Valais, now winter-bare. It answered his longing for 'a room of my own, with a few old things and a window opening onto great trees'. Dark oak beams spanned the ceiling, low enough to make him duck instinctively as he paced about, though he was not tall. Beside the window was a standing-desk, made exactly to his specifications, at which he always wrote. In this room, as he had pledged in 1906, he would 'kneel down and stand up daily', alone, 'and keep holy all that befalls me.'

All was in order. He was ready. The candlestick on the bookcase, the new glass-lidded box for tacks and pens razor-straight on the table, the porcelain vase standing exactly where it had stood before, though it held no roses now, for those were past, or yet to come. Somewhere on the bookshelves lay a French prose version of Ovid's *Metamorphoses*, recently reread. Rilke had been steeping himself again in the story of Orpheus, the magician-singer of the ancient world, his love for Eurydice and his descent to Hades to rescue her. A Renaissance engraving of Orpheus by Cima da Conegliano, reproduced on a postcard, was also pinned over his desk. Merline had spotted it in a local shop. It showed a young man in page's clothes, under a spreading tree, singing sadly to a *lira da braccio* while two deer listened. It reminded Rilke, though he needed no reminding, of his mission as a poet.

It also helped preserve the memory of a young friend, Vera Knoop, who had died two months before. She was nineteen, and had suffered from a baffling glandular disease. For years she had astonished people with her dancing and her 'dark, strange, fiery loveliness' until, at the end of childhood, she suddenly told her mother that she would not dance any more. In her last weeks Orpheus had begun to haunt her: invisibly playing music to which she raised her tired, wasting arms, gently pushing the pencil with which she tried, wearily, to draw.

But Rilke would not think of her this morning. He was trying to finish a great symphony of poetry, his *Duino Elegies*, which sang of the sublime, violent interaction between angels and men. After ten years of neglecting it, inspiration was beginning to stir again. He dared not risk losing or unsettling it.

Consciously empty yet anticipating something, 'wrapping myself more and more closely round my heart', he took up his station at the standing-desk.

And suddenly, Orpheus was there.

The singer of singers. To Rilke he needed no introduction; to us, perhaps, he does. We demand a curriculum vitae, a flyer or a calling card. Instead he brings music and the wind with him, and no information.

His origins are lost. In the beginning he was perhaps a vegetation god, a deity of growth, death and resurrection. Hence 'Orpheus', by one derivation: dark, obscure, out of the earth. But godhead gradually slipped away from him, leaving only a sense of election and the power, through his music, to change landscapes, seasons, hearts.

To the Thracians, among whom perhaps he really lived thirty centuries ago, he was a king, a shaman and a traveller through the realms of the dead. To the ancient Greeks he was the first singer of holy songs and the founder of their mysteries, an enchanter who could make the stones skip, the trees dance and birds waver in the air. (He still can; ask him.) He was the companion of the Argonauts and their priest on the voyage to find the Golden Fleece: a teacher of beauty and order who was eventually torn apart, in Thrace, by followers of the wine god Dionysus and devotees of chaos.

By the fifth century BC he had acquired a wife, Eurydice, and when she died he went down to Hades, armed only with music, to bargain for her with the rulers of the Underworld. But the Greeks hardly cared for this part of his story. It was the Romans, especially Ovid and Virgil in their poetry, who made of him a lover so ardent that he challenged death. Both his love and his art were pitted against annihilation, and though he failed, they became immortal. That is mostly why the world remembers him.

In this guise of sweet singer, lover and loser, Orpheus has wandered through history. Poets, artists and composers have constantly evoked this figure, and still do. But the teacher and philosopher was not forgotten by Renaissance Florence or the nineteenth-century theosophists; the magician and spell-binder, familiar to the Greeks, was remembered by alchemists until Newton's time; his adventure in Hell was allegorised as the journey of the soul by Boethius in the sixth century AD, as well as by Freud and Jung in the twentieth. For at least sixteen centuries Christians easily imagined him, with his miracles and parables, his redeeming power and his bloody, sacrificial death, as a forerunner of Jesus, though preaching with song in the forests of ancient Greece rather than the deserts of Judaea.

To some degree you could argue that each age revisits him. Yet none puts its stamp on him definitively, because the young man with the lyre is different for everyone who meets him. Each encounter makes him anew, until it is clear that the vulnerable human figure still conceals his most primal incarnation: the pulse of creation, the song of life, then, now, always.

Perhaps you have heard his footstep – perhaps Rilke heard it. But it is rare to do so. His feet are bare, or strapped in light sandals, or cased in boots of soft fawn-skin turned over at the top in the Thracian style. The leather is thin because he needs to tap the ground, or feel it, as he plays. And it is thin because he has journeyed so far towards us.

Greek Orpheus is naked but for a *chlamys*, a short cloak, which usually drapes him from the waist. It has no certain colour, though poets think it blue. His head is uncovered, his long dark ringlets held back with a wreath of laurel, or ribbon, or gold thread. In his eastern guise he wears a striped dalmatic over baggy trousers and a gold *tiara*, or Persian turban, the mark of a prince. Thracian Orpheus wears leggings stitched along the side-seam, a warm, thick cloak clasped at the right shoulder and a cone-shaped Phrygian cap, proper to wanderers, countrymen and radicals, that is often revolutionary red and sometimes sown with stars.

The first mention you will find of him, and the earliest certain painting, date from the sixth century BC. The painting, in black-figure on a Greek vase, shows him stepping up to a platform with pointed toe, dancing, in a pleated robe and with a huge lyre that seems to be part of him. The lettering around the figure cries 'Hail, Orpheus'. The written fragment, by Ibycus, calls him 'famous'. As far back as we can trace Orpheus he is celebrated, a star. In fact, he may have been pictured long before he was named: on a clay vase from Crete of the thirteenth century BC, and on a plaque of the same age from Syria-Palestine. On each his lyre was oversized, denoting divine power; on both, charmed birds flew to his playing, as if drawn down by magnets from the sky. The Cretan vase showed him crested and beaked, a bird himself, or an avatar of song.

He has never left men's consciousness since. But it is a strange sort of haunting. The evidence for him lies in tiny fragments: a line here, a mention there, *dubia vel spuria*, as the scholars say. Orpheus roams Western civilisation much as balladeers, hurdy-gurdy men, pipers and storytellers used to travel the back roads of America and Europe. Possibly he has come even further, from ancient India, where a god of hunting or fishing spread a net that became a lyre of enchantment, to catch men's souls. He has no certain roots, but keeps returning, as if he has something urgent to transmit to us.

Inevitably, his home is out of doors. He needs, as Rilke put it once, 'the open country, wide ways, barefoot wanderings on soft grass, on hard roads or pure snow, deep breathing, listening, silence and the hush of evening'. He never stays. He is a shadow in the doorway, a face outside the window in the night rain, begging not for bread or coins, but for attention. When we hear him, time stops and for a moment everything is changed; but then he moves on.

Homer's epics never included him. Aristotle said he had

never lived. Cicero wrote as though he agreed, calling Orpheus's hymns 'fairy stories'. 'Now how', he added, 'can I form a mental picture of someone who has never existed? Yet Orpheus, or the image of him, often enters my mind.' Socrates, about to drink the hemlock, mused joyfully on the possibility of talking with him in Hades. It was precisely because Orpheus was a proper, flesh-and-blood man 'and not a wind', wrote Claudio Monteverdi, that people were moved by his story. Hard proof was always lacking. But in truth he existed – he exists – wherever he is thought of, believed in or imagined. Chaucer saw him in his House of Fame, sitting in a niche in a turret of pure beryl, playing 'ful craftely'; Wordsworth saw him in 1806 in Oxford Street, his back to a sooty wall, playing the violin to a crowd of apprentices, cripples and bakers' boys, 'twenty souls happy / As souls in a dream'. As Rilke was to write of the unicorn, at Orpheus's dictation, 'It *was* not, but love / brought it to be, and men always left space for it.' They left space for him.

His face may be a man's or a boy's; you cannot tell. It bears a youthful fuzz of stubble, the cynosure of male beauty for the Greeks, but also the lines of grief and experience. His eyes are deep as pools, and watchful; his eyebrows thick, his nose straight. You will notice his hands, fine, strong, long-fingered, as a pianist's are: the nails trimmed squarely, the knuckles tested and flexed, and with a sense of fluttering movement in them, even at rest. A quick pencil line will catch him, as Jean Cocteau drew him for the opening frames of his film *Orphée* in 1950, joining dot to dot to make his profile, finishing with a star. Or a thin brush will snare him, moistened with spittle and dipped in black paint, on the curve of a terracotta vase. Near the Temple of the Winds in Athens is a shop with dozens of such vases, of every size, stacked among the Acropolis T-shirts and the football flags that stir in the breeze from the hot, dog-wandered street. You may buy a perfect Orpheus there, and then a better and still better one, his bent black head outlined with white, his dark eye serious, and with strange heart-shaped laurel leaves garlanding his hair. In a smoke-filled room not far away, men and women are painting more, on an oilcloth-covered table under a flickering TV screen. Brow, nose, chin, the singing mouth, the hands, the lyre.

That face was drawn throughout the Roman Empire, on door jambs and tympanums, in bedrooms, on garden walls. Philostratus the younger, walking through a gallery in Naples around AD 240, paused to admire a painting of him:

> Orpheus sits there, the down of a first beard spreading on his cheeks, a *tiara* bright with gold tall on his head, his eye tender, yet alert and divinely inspired as his mind ever reaches out to divine themes. Perhaps even now he is singing a song; indeed his eyebrow seems to indicate the sense of what he sings, and his robe changes colour with his movements . . .

Orpheus with a charmed stag was painted in the Domus Aurea, Nero's palace, and his face was on the red-gloss trays; Hadrian had a mural of him captivating Cerberus, the three-headed dog-guardian of the Underworld. But he was also on the beechwood cups carved for the shepherd Damoetas in Virgil's *Eclogues*: cups far too fine to drink from, offered as a singing prize, kept under lock and key in a smoky cottage in the hills. His image was on rings, wine vessels, mirrors, plates and medallions. It appeared on coins struck in Thrace, his supposed country, and in Alexandria, where some thought he had studied.

Most of all, from the mid-second century, it was laid in villa floors. His face was made of tiny tesserae piled, arranged and grouped by colour: black for the outline, red for the open, singing lips, white and brown for the eyes that stared on divine things. At Arae Flaviae (now Rottweil, in south-western Germany) 750,000 tesserae were ordered to make his long white robe, his cloak clasped at the shoulder, his pale hands plucking the lyre and his glance, tender, passionate and surprised, at the raven listening to him. The workmen whistled; Orpheus appeared. Though long ago he had been dismembered, he was reconstructed and he lived. In mosaics at Brading on the Isle of Wight, Palermo, Jerusalem, Woodchester on the Welsh borders, Paphos, Hanover, Tarsus, Sparta and Vienna he plays still, the plectrum in his right hand, the strings set ringing with his left, while animals circle around him. He is so ubiquitous that it would be no surprise, taking the path through a little wood near Sudeley in Gloucestershire where Roman floors still lie beneath the brambles, to find in a timber cloche, under a tarpaulin, the leaves dark and crowding overhead, his singing face.

His eyes seldom look at you. When he sings, he stares heavenwards; at rest, his glance is elsewhere. Rilke, though gradually possessed by Orpheus – unable to leave his standing-desk for that pressure, that presence – feels and hears him, rather than endures his gaze. Atheneus called him a 'semi-god', but he seems too shy for that: polite but removed, by choice a loner. No vanity is in him, as far as appearance goes. He does not look in mirrors, though he knows what they show is true: the self and the world seen from the other side, by clear-eyed Death. Mirrors belong on his altars, objects of ritual and respect. He wears no ornaments, save perhaps a ring of agate engraved with a tree, which, by his own account, will make him pleasing to the gods. He can never be too pleasing, never too close.

Little seems essential to him. He carries no provisions for his wanderings, and if they are offered he will probably refuse them. A piece of sooty, flaky barley-cake, fresh out of the fire, and a cup of water are all he requires. Food impairs the voice, obstructs the throat; he prefers to sing and practise fasting, with just a swallow of milk and honey, holy food, to give the smoothness he needs. He abstains from the eggs of birds as 'living things', though his imagery of the beginning of creation is the cloudy membrane of an egg breaking, spilling out light. Wine he sips only as a cautious, meditative act, since the mixing of wine and water in the bowl is a metaphor for the creation of mortal things; or because it represents the cup of wisdom and self-surrender offered to souls, if they will drink. Hand him an apple, as Rilke was to do, and it will become – as if by magic – a totem of invisible things: a tree at the edge of the Libyan desert, and a nymph's raised white arms; a memory of a table, a bowl, the play of the light, in another place; a shiver of *Tod und Leben*, death and life, as the hard flesh is crushed into sweetness. He turns it into mind-food, as poets do. Only after this, which is the work of a moment, will he eat it in the ordinary way.

Meat he refuses, both as food and offering, because the gods do not need blood sacrifices – and because meat-eating, like flute-playing, binds a man to the sensual world. While others slice meat on bread, he prefers a little thyme, or cress, or saltwort. He stays cool, while others are heated or excited by eating flesh. Beans he abominates, believing that they corrupt the breath of the body (turning it into a hollow, trumpeting pipe of filth) and seeing them, with their twisting stems and white moon-flowers, as ways for the ancestral dead to climb back to the upper world. He does not wear wool, because it is the coat of something living. His taboos seem as capricious as a teenager's, or as those of some Pacific islander who will not sleep beneath the breadfruit tree because of some ancient, half-remembered curse. But he has barricaded them behind philosophy, and he holds fast to them.

Above all he carries his lyre, a hollow shell with curved arms and a cross-bar, strung with seven strings. It is perhaps the very one first made by Hermes, the trickster-god, its mottled shell shiny with use and the dark gut strings mellow to his touch. Or it is Apollo's, the sun god's own instrument, of gold fretted with ivory, as the Greeks imagined. It contains all poetry and all songs. It is engraved, with broken strings, on the tombstone of Keats; it decorated the box that held Haydn's skull; it represents all poets, all trees and the world itself, when the divine wind plays. With this cradled in his arm or hanging from its travelling strap, he needs no eye contact and no words. He may play softly even as you talk to him, too absorbed for ordinary chatter. Music feeds him. His lyre has grown into his body like another layer of the heart. They beat together.

This would have been the first sound he heard: his mother's heart, deep and regular, through the walls of the womb. By tradition she was Calliope, 'beautiful-voiced', the loveliest and first of the nine Muses, Memory's daughters. She was a singer of epic poems and creation-hymns whose melodies, too, he would have heard in the blood. After the cataclysm of his first breath, the slap on his back, the swift singer's baptism of honey smeared on his lips, those songs would surround him again, closer and louder now, as he nuzzled the breast. They pulsed in his ears with the first sweet flow of milk into his softly plugged mouth. In fifteenth-century Scotland, Robert Henryson imagined it:

> Quhen he was borne schoe set him on hir kne
> And gart him sowke of hir twa palpis quhyte
> The sweit licour of all musike parfyte.

Afterwards, laid down in some womb-dark cave or chamber of an enchanted mountain, he heard more. The fire hissing; the creak of his cradle; a caged bird above him, whose swirl of notes caused his tiny body to jerk, clench and start. Round the entrance of the cave the wind blew with a sound as solicitous as breathing.

Exactly where this happened was unknown. It was assumed to be in Thrace, north of Greece, in that inhospitable region of plain and mountain wedged between the Danube and the Aegean: on Mount Pangaion, or Mount Helicon, or the Pierian heights where the Muses lived, all peaks on the Greek side of the Rhodope mountains that were linked to inspiration, and to him. Yet the south-central region of the Rhodopes, now in modern Bulgaria, claims him most passionately. To the people here – the man with a hoe on horseback, tickling his steed with a leafing branch, the girl in glasses driving a dirt-spattered cow, the old woman in a sunhat, pausing on a forest road with her arms full of roses – these are 'Orpheus's mountains'. On road signs, his lyre is shorthand for him. Here a cobbled Orpheus Street runs up the hillside among rusty Ladas and wild cats; there an Orpheus Restaurant tempts you, with drifting wood-smoke and a new Coca-Cola sign; there, at the Orpheus Resort and Spa, he plays beside an ornamental pool that is domed and blue-tiled like a Persian palace. At Shiroka Luka he sings from the wall of the music school, while at Kardzhali his lyre, in angular steel tubing, stands at the main crossroads. But it is tiny Gela, four miles from Shiroka Luka up a steeply winding road, that claims the honour of his birth-place. Perhaps eighty souls live here, in a handful of houses in high alpine meadows rimmed by castellated mountains. Every year they hold a bagpipe-playing contest in which satyr-music swirls again round the slopes of Mount Orpheus, named in his honour. And at the highest point of the village, in a grassy playground with a tyre-swing, low football nets and an abandoned Soviet army truck, Orpheus's lyre made from logs and string catches the wind from the valley, while the Bulgarian flag flaps behind it.

So much for where. But when his childhood happened was even more mysterious. According to one of Orpheus's 'own' books, *Lithica*, or *On Stones*, in which (Diodorus said) he 'revealed a little about himself', he seemed to have been born about a generation before Homer, around 800 BC, though when Homer had lived was also cloudy. In the age of the heroes Orpheus sang alongside them, teaching Heracles and sailing with him on the *Argo* to fetch the Golden Fleece. Plato, in his *Laws* of 350 BC or so, thought Orpheus's 'discoveries' had been made 'one or two thousand years ago'. That sort of date, around the thirteenth century BC, was favoured centuries later by Bulgarian archaeologists who felt sure he had really lived. But it was never quite as simple as that. His name, with its ending in –eus, suggested that he belonged to an age the Greeks con - sidered mythical. Both the Sibyl and Moses were said to be old when he was born; but then both music and language seemed to be very young. Time slipped and slid around him, unanchored by any fact that could be verified. Perhaps it did not matter. 'Where does our story take place, and when?' asked Cocteau at the start of *Orphée*. 'It's the privilege of legends to be ageless. *Comme il vous plaira*. As you please.'

Nature taught him in his earliest days, with sounds he alone seemed to hear. To his child's ears, everything was amplified. A drop of water, trickling in a grotto, made a note shriller and sharper than a drop falling to the earth. The stream beneath the banks, half-caught in overhanging stems, sang more noisily than the open water. He described the nymphs swimming, 'oblique' and 'swift-soaring' in the chanting current, with light cascading through their bodies: light he could not catch, although he tried to. More nymphs haunted the grass, where a small child could find them, or flickered in damp openings in the rocks, 'visible and invisible'. He saw the dew that clothed them and heard their high, faint song before they vanished, 'travellers of the winding roads', white limbs into white air.

Above him the firs of the forest sent out high, sighing plaints, while the broad oaks sang leafier and low. Rain and thunder made colossal battle-music, grey doves the sound of sleep, the owl of the night-shades one keen, swooping interval that pierced his heart. It was generally believed, said Theophilus, that Orpheus learned his music from the birds. His small voice, piping after theirs, filled with all the secret stories of the earth. In summer the invisible cicadas sang their two-note dirge, surviving from the time before music came into the world. He could also hear the spider spinning notes higher and further as its web stretched out between the thistle stalks, pulled from its own innermost heart, diamonded with dew. At the edge of the grasslands, music passed from tasselled reed to reed as the wind sighed through them. He heard fruits rounding on the branch, flower-stems unsheathing from the soil; the creak and tinkle of ice feathering across a pool, and the fall, note by hushed note, of the snow. Beneath it all hummed the tone of the mountains in their jagged majesty, the bass-line of his life.

He was given his lyre when he was still a child, barely taller than the frame. Calliope, steadying him, showed him how to chant like her as he played. All his poet's art, and much of his mystic wisdom, was apparently learned from her. Her hair was loosed from its dark wreath of ivy as she sang, falling over him in waves like the long, silvered leaves of the willows by the river. Music was also mother-comfort, enfolding him in the soft thrill of the mother-voice. By her singing, he knew, the nine daughters of Pierus had been turned into chattering magpies, flashing white, blue and black in the garden before they flew into the bowl of the sky.

In particular (Homer thought) Calliope sang of Apollo, god of song and the sun: his eyes alight beneath his golden helmet, his face and hair radiating glory, bright Aether robing him in fire. With Aether's golden chains, Orpheus sang later, Apollo bound the world as Zeus bound all creation. It was not the usual small child's rhyme; but he was no ordinary child.

Apollo may even have taught him, as the god himself had been taught by Hermes. The little Thracian boy, twirling joyously in some patch of forest sun, held up his arms to the song god, who gave him an instrument that thrilled with his own brightness. Rainbows clung to it, breaking out of the white glare. Rays became strings, with sacred song encoded in them. A golden hand seized his fingers, crooking them the right way around a plectrum edged with light. Mysteries were passed down, as well as music. But this he was to understand later.

Some thought Apollo was in fact his father, and he a sun-child. This was the earliest story of his origin. If it was true, he may have learned from him the giving of oracles, the taming of eagles, the luring of wild beasts, and how to heal. In his *Lithica* Orpheus was explicitly Apollo's son, leaping always and instantly to his command to 'sing a poet's song out of my breast'. But Apollo had human failings too, and even human experience. For a year, as a punishment, he had tended sheep for a human master. He loved unwisely, was frightened, raged, wept. Orpheus often came across his tears, streaking the petals of wild larkspur or shining as beads of amber on far-away shores. The sun god wept over the world to which he had been forced to descend. But, like a mortal, he could do nothing to change the Fate that had been spun for him.

As commonly, Orpheus's father was said to be Oeagros, King of Thrace. His name meant variously 'the hunter', 'the sheep-herder' or 'the lone dweller in the fields'. The incongruity of this boorish, rustic father was caught by Jean Anouilh in his play *Eurydice* of 1942: he made Oeagros a second-rate travelling harpist totting up his receipts in a railway café, while his elegant, high-minded son played the violin beside him. Somehow, a Muse had taken a human for a lover. No physical evidence firmly connected Orpheus to the country that Oeagros ruled over; he might more plausibly have been, as *The Sandman* graphic series made him in the 1990s, the son of Oneiros or Morpheus, the god of dreams. But in sixth- and fifth-century Greek imaginations Thrace was always his, the strange and distant 'other' place, the winter-land.

From the end of the sixth century BC – just as Orpheus himself emerged by name in the world – a royal house and a warrior aristocracy had come into existence there, drawing their wealth from the wide eastern plains. Gold vessels and masks of astonishing beauty, some traded, some looted, some home-produced, were buried with Thracian kings in towering earth mounds. Contacts with Greece brought in bronze and silver wine-vessels, wine itself, Greek fashion in dress and ornament, and the use of written and spoken Greek at court. Fifth-century Athenians made Orpheus something like this, half-Thracian and half-Greek. According to Iamblichus, he spoke Doric, the oldest and best of the Greek dialects, with ringing enharmonic tones that coloured both speech and music. But he could equally be imagined, with a northern twang, playing with boys called Tralis, Skindax or Tokes, ruddy-faced and red-haired, like most Thracians. As a boy of noble birth he was branded, though in Greece that was the mark of slaves; whether or not he was the sun's son, he might wear a wreath of delicate gold leaves and tattoos of sun-discs on his arms.

His father's subjects lived in one-room huts or chambers underground, the walls lined with clay or wolf-skins. Rough hemp made their clothes; their leggings chafed them as they moved. They used grey pottery, with high looped handles and zigzag patterns, and fastened their cloaks on the shoulder with double-looped bronze *fibulae*, or safety-pin clasps, as Orpheus usually wore his. Their diet was mares' milk and barley-bread, greyish and full of chaff. They worshipped Ares, the war god, Artemis, the moon goddess of light, and Dionysus, the god of growth and vines, whose cult had started either in Thrace or in Crete. They loved war, and were given to drinking sessions where barley-beer or unmixed wine was quaffed out of horns in a single breath, 'Thracian-fashion'.

The Odrysians and Bistonians were the tribes that Oeagros traditionally ruled over. He taught them mystic rites, Diodorus said, and passed these on to his 'quite exceptional' son. But he was also at times a wine god, at times the god of the sorb-apple tree, and on occasion the god of the River Hebrus that flowed through his own cold kingdom, past the green swan-haunted banks where Orpheus played.

That son may have been the only good thing to come out of Thrace. Virgil and Ovid both agreed that there was nothing worth praising in the grassy plains and the cold, lowering mountains. 'The cattle are kept in the stalls there,' shivered Virgil:

Not a blade of grass appears on the plain, not a leaf on the
  trees;
But as far as the eye can reach the earth lies, her features
  lost
Beneath snowdrifts and ice to a depth of seven fathoms.
It's always winter, always the cold nor'-easter blowing.
And worse, the sun can never break through the wan
  gloom there –
Not when his horses draw him up to the height of heaven,
Not when his chariot brings him to bathe in the blood-red
  sea.

The Pirin and Rhodopes ranges, which bordered the
immense steppe, were crusted half the year with snow. Firs,
pines and hornbeam covered the northern slopes of the
mountains, pines and oak the southern. Six varieties of oak
grew in the forest: the broad-leaved *Quercus pubescens*, with
leaves easily twisted into garlands, became Orpheus's sacred
tree. Thyme perfumed the barer places. At times clouds lay
below the pine-clad peaks, misting off them in bright white
plumes as though they were on fire. Hermits and wanderers
also lived in the forest, 'walkers on smoke' who kept to a
diet of cheese, milk, honey and narcotic plants, and who
knew healing charms. They sang as they wandered the stone-
strewn paths. Thracian shamans were famous before Orpheus,
linking the worlds of the living and the dead and surviving
beyond the grave as *anthropodaimones*, man-daemons. They
observed the stars, knew their names and courses, and could
predict their effect on men. When the gods possessed them
they could fly through the clouds, and dive under the sea;

they could charm wild beasts and birds, whose language they knew; and from time to time they went down to the Underworld to summon out souls, or so it was believed.

Below the mountains the vast grasslands produced mostly barley and bitter weeds. Herdsmen and hunters roamed over them, driving through the winter blizzards scattering and thundering columns of wild horses. The word *Thrax* or Thracian, applied to a Roman racehorse, meant savage, barbarian, untouchable. This was a landscape of illusions, pale horizons and far-fading herds. When snow fell, 'the air one white drift', in Virgil's words, Thracians thought of it as feathers shaken out of the sky. Two things all commentators noticed: the cold, the horses.

This might have explained the strange, lingering power of an image Rilke recorded in the spring of 1900. He was in a meadow by the Volga, in deepest Russia, at evening. Before him lay a paddock at the edge of the steppe, a wooden fence, and a small white stallion running with a hobble on its leg. Something about the horse – its joyous eagerness, the flopping white mane, its half-vanishing gallop in the twilight – instinctively made him offer the scene, twenty-two years later, as an *ex-voto* to Orpheus. As his insistent young visitor took him over, he suddenly recalled it:

> Oh how he felt, was inspired by space,
> sang, heard, *was* your song through
> and through.
> I dedicate this image to you.

Rilke may not have known, or not remembered, that white horses were sacred to Apollo; or that when God walked the earth as a wandering musician, knocking on farm doors in the dark as the Russians believed, the first intimation of him was of animals stirring, and the thud of hooves in the night grass.

Half-brothers vaguely entered the picture of Orpheus's early life: other boys fathered by Apollo and associated, like him, with fields and trees, melancholy and sweetness. One was Aristeus, a bee-keeper, later to appear in his story as a rival in love and a blue-cloaked betrayer. The other was Linus, a shepherd-poet who died young. He was mourned in lamentations for the death of plants under the summer sun, or for the end of summer itself: the first music, some said, from human tears. He wore a crown of flowers and parsley with its flat, bitter leaves. The boy Orpheus was casually coupled with them sometimes, but he was already walking alone. Certain ancient mosaics distinguished him from Apollo by showing him not with a menagerie of animals, charmed by his playing, but with a lone, curious fox.

He was possibly named from the alder, a tree of damp, waste places. It stood beside water and, when cut with the double-axe, bled crimson like a man. That made it also a tree of resurrection, death-and-life. Sinewy alder wood was used for double pipes; perhaps he played them, since they made music of a sort, as grass blades did when he blew them between his small cupped hands. But he already knew that such music was lower, sensuous, of the body; that recorders were the sound of shepherd life, and that crude flutes were played when the stallion covered the mare. His lyre, whether goat-horn or golden, made the music of some higher place.

He was full of curious knowledge, even as a child. Diodorus said he devoted his whole boyhood to learning, especially 'whatever the myths had to say about the gods'. He learned their names and epithets, how they moved, what they did, not forgetting to add the word 'blessed' whenever he spoke of them. He knew the colour of their eyes, the weight of their footsteps, their speed in the cosmos and their traces on the earth. Zeus Thunderbolt, who shocked him with angry god-tears crashing down from heaped black clouds; laughing Aphrodite, born from the foam of the far-distant sea, who wove everything together in love; motherly Demeter, crowned with bending barley, who gave perfumed red nectar to the gods and sticky honey-cakes to him; Artemis, the moon, whose white face filled the night window and silvered the sleeping trees. No one knew who taught him. It was assumed he learned without scrolls, books or slates, since letters came later. He simply listened, perhaps to the deities themselves.

He was to sing sometimes, tenderly, of the childhoods of the gods: of little Zeus, the all-creator, hidden in a thyme-scented Cretan cave that suckled him with water from its limestone teats, his cries drowned by the guardian Kouretes clashing their shields; or of wine god Dionysus in his cradle of a willow winnowing-basket swaying from the tree, with baby-toys around him:

> cone, and spinning top, rattles, jointed dolls,
> and fair golden apples from the sweet-voiced Hesperides.

These playthings formed part of the mystic ceremonies Orpheus later organised, neatly assembled on the altar. He added knucklebone dice, a ball, a hoop, a mirror of polished bronze.

All these objects had symbolic significance by then. Golden apples, possibly quinces, were a memento of mystical journeys and ordeals; puppets, jerking on strings, scared spirits away; the ball was the shining earth-globe set spinning by Eros or baby Zeus, its golden zones stitched invisibly and spiralled with the dark-blue sea. The shining mirror, held up to his face and touched with searching fingers, would show him the other side of life, as it had lured the child Dionysus to a place where Death embraced him. His 'cone' was a sort of top, wound round with cord, which made the unheard whirr of the sun moving, or the beat of Dionysus's torn-out heart. And last of all came a spinner, the 'bull-roarer', a disc of wood on a long string whirled around his head as fast as he could until it howled with the songs of all the demons on the steppe, coming to pull him apart.

He realised very young what music could do. It could capture wild creatures as deftly as his hunter-father, but without spears, or snares, or blood. By the Aegean shore lived fishermen who, with their pipes, could charm fish into the shallows and catch them there in nets. He, with his lyre, by a stream, could pluck a note and watch the fish grow still. Their silent pink mouths opened, as though to take the hook of the sound; their bodies stiffened, no longer twisting but merely rippling with colour, rainbow scale to scale, as they idled in the water. They were alive, yet entranced, and by palace pools he could play his lyre deliberately to collect the golden carp like dead leaves or long-scaled pine-cones, glittering and floating up from the depths. In later times some deduced from his name that he was a fisher of men, or their souls.

He sang in the mountain meadows, too, and was aware that the scene would subtly start to adjust itself. Stone moved against stone, or a life that was not a bird flared suddenly in bush or tree – near, far, red, blue – to the tunes he made. Everything, as he looked at it, came alive. The birds themselves flew close, silent and bright-eyed, as if he had somehow snared them, claw and wing, without a net. They perched on his naked shoulder, thistledown with just a prick of claws. He could pick them up, observing how each light, warm cage of feathers pulsed softly, but did not sing. They let him sing for them. Around him the undergrowth crackled and stirred, as if a forest fire was in it. You might see him in these meadows in summer, a half-naked boy with tanned, golden skin stepping like a dancer and holding his lyre aloft, out of danger, away from the flaming, rearing grass.

One day as he played a stream followed him. It rose first above the stones of its usual bed, shimmering faster and higher, then swelled through the reeds and grasses at his feet, dribbling and trickling after him like a shadow, like a cat, awaiting his instructions. He led it to a rounded overhanging rock to watch it feel and spread its way across, braiding brightly as it went, a net of water, then let it fall through empty air to the tangled scrub, to the looped, prickling brambles, to the astonished earth. When he scrambled down, it gushed from the soaking bushes into his hands.

He could also make the water stop. Quiet, long notes, and even the wide Hebrus would begin to flatten, to sink like a concave glass and then retreat, sucked back into its dry whitish bed with a silvery flick, like a fish. Then he could bring it out again, beckoning and flickering his fingers on the strings. His own music seemed to be water's sound and light, flashing in star-bursts underneath the trees. Beside mountain streams he played its pealing, dripping, funnelling flow, and the spark-note of bubbles bursting; he plucked its underwater gulp among shadowed stones, and the bright plaited threads that twined as it fell. He played its foaming surge through slipping, moss-slick rocks, he and Nature together. You whirl the world, he sang to Nature later:

> circling in all, your ever-changing flow
> rushing and swirling to each stream below,
> and nothing slows the force with which you go.

In pools still as mirrors he observed his own body, spun like a veil or a net on the 'marble loom' of his bones: the blue veins branching, his hair raying in a vortex from the crown of his head, his navel a deep shell. All this seemed fluid to him, rather than flesh. Jumping off into the water, kicking his feet, swimming, he became a naked helix of gleaming, winding waves. All his teachings, some said later, could be summed up in a single word: *rheo*, I flow away.

Yet at the same time he could be still, shining, in trance. His music calmed him, too, and slowed his blood, even as he played. His inner power was undisturbed even when, before dawn, a wild white horse stepping from the shadowy mist shocked him into silence. Something seemed to bind him then, as Apollo with his golden chains bound the world and tamed it. The animal most often placed beside him was the gentle hind, also Apollo's creature, sometimes collared and leashed although neither was necessary, drawn thirsting from the woods to the water and the light.

The source of both stillness and desire he eventually called soul. Most men in that dawn of philosophy saw it as a misty life-breath, mere smoke that fled when the body died. He believed it was the radiant and boundless essence of a man, dwelling within the sacred head or the pulsing heart like fire. He determined much later that a membrane of coarse fibres, an imprisoning husk, had meshed around it as it descended. Life and Fate were spun together. Souls travelled, he sang, in the gusts of the wind, falling out of Aether to be breathed in by newborn humans from the air. Night revealed them as shooting stars, showered down in music, till they were trapped in the prison of the world:

> Round about a cloud has settled
> in the dense and thickening air.
> Mortal eyes have mortal pupils.
> Only flesh and bones grow there.

Through these eyes, however, the soul still tried to see; smothered in the air, always thick and dark to him, it struggled to feed its own wavering flame; and through his lyre, even with searching, childish tunes, it tried to sing. All the beauty he saw – from the solitary blue gentian on a hillside to a tier of clouds, their fiery tops brushed out in evening light – came to him with music, though unheard by anyone else. His soul leapt towards it like remembrance.

Only one incident was recorded from his childhood. He related it in the *Lithica*. As he roamed in the mountains one day – out to catch birds, focused only on that one thing – he encountered a dragon-snake, coiled, cold, its huge jaws opening already, about to strike him. He raced to take refuge in a sanctuary of Apollo, where sappy branches still lay unburned among the ashes on the altar. It was perhaps the womb-shaped artificial cave near Kardzhali where, each day at noon, some chink or opening in the rock will let a ray of sun strike through, like a sword. He grabbed a branch to beat the serpent as its head and neck writhed after him, almost into the cave, then dashed for the open air. His father Apollo had sent two white hunting dogs to protect him. He let them bait the serpent while, breathless and trembling, he crept among a group of sheep sheltering in the rocks. Their warm, oily wool concealed him until it was safe to move again.

Through Nature, gradually, Orpheus became the first of poets and the foremost of musicians. He followed the divine Mother – Rhea, or Physis, as he most often called her – and watched how she made the green shoots appear, spiralling and rotating out of the dark earth, in patterns that never varied but endlessly multiplied; how she made the yellow sprays of the sycamore or the red-silver tufts of the oak unfold and spread, and the bearded barley turn until it quivered like copper in the fields. Grass, flowers and trees, he sang, were woven over the earth like a robe. And Physis herself was sheer motive force, soft, subtle, shining:

> Swift is the motion of your feet and your steps noiseless,
> O pure marshal of the gods, end that has no end.
> All share in you but you partake of no one,
> self-fathered and hence fatherless; lovely, joyous, great,
>   our friend,
> you nurse the flowers, you mingle and twine in love . . .

The god Dionysus also walked where she did, spreading like his own sacred vine and stirring in all green life. In Thrace he was a version of a god, much more ancient, who was summoned every spring from where he slumbered under the roots and the grass. Hollow drums roused him from the hollow earth. This god could be seen in trees, with a man's limbs and, under the bark, a man's bearded face. Slabs of honey-comb and necklaces of dried figs were draped around him; little images were hung in the branches to propitiate him, glinting and swinging like the catkins of spring.

All things flowered and died again. In Orpheus's later ceremonies green branches were given to worshippers to remind them of the fruiting earth and the brevity of forms. In his own words: 'All things turn around and must go full circle, and it is not lawful to stand still.' Neither life nor beauty could be motionless. Everything grew, divided, faded, flowed away:

> and as the fruitful field produces blades,
> and on the ash some leaves fade, others grow,
> so whirls the race of men . . .

Seneca summed up his songs in one remark: 'Nothing that is made lasts for ever.'

Despite his love of learning, Orpheus evidently drew most lessons from the open air. Like John Clare's herding and foddering boys, sauntering beside brooks, swaddled in scarves against the crunching snow, hunting snail-shells under the hedge, he filled his days in the woods and fields. His hymns revelled in 'the sweet breath of grass, the joy of the rain'. In the *Lithica* he lay under shady elm trees, face-down in the green. The horses cropped as he dreamed. Ovid filled 'his' songs with close observation: the droop of poppy heads on their thin stems, the leathery skin of pomegranates that held, like a purse, the blood-red seeds, the clustering yellow stamens of lilies and the 'silver-whiteness' of their petals. Orpheus would have picked pink and scarlet anenomes ('so fragile, the petals so lightly attached, the wind shakes them away') and pulled down the swirling wreaths of wild clematis as if they were there only for him, and he was the first boy to see them. And in a way he was.

The poet's task, as Rilke had written once, was 'so deeply and painfully and passionately to impress upon ourselves this provisional and perishable Earth, that its essential being will rise again "invisible" in us. We are the bees of the invisible, wildly plundering the visible of its honey.' So Orpheus plundered. He stowed what he saw in mind and heart to shine with an intenser light, and out of that light he sang. He had a phrase, mentioned by Plato in his *Laws*, for clear-sighted, child-like joy: 'when delight in life is in its springtime'.

Perhaps even now he is singing a song.

*

At Pamporovo, thirty miles north-east of Gela, the Murvetz Grand Hotel is holding a music night. In late September, out of season, only two hotels are open in this skiing place, the Murvetz and the Orlovetz, with perhaps two dozen guests between them. Business is quiet for the old man in the car-park, with white stubble and his arms full of cow-bells. ('Buy the whole set! *Complet, complet!* Do-re-mi!') The Orpheus Hotel is closed, even though he stands in bronze outside it, a boy with cupped hands raised to sing like a bird, in case the tourists hear him.

All around lie the forests and the peaks, utterly quiet. Once or twice a woodpecker calls; a wild dog barks, setting off the others; then silence descends again. Walk up a gravel track, past the casino sign, and you will pass on the right a row of shops without fittings, still half-built; a hotel that displays, through dusty windows, a waterless swimming pool; and, in the deeper woods, two hotel corpses, crushed to rubble under their collapsed concrete roofs and with rusty electric cables writhing out like the roots of dead, ice-ravaged trees, as if an avalanche has passed. Around them, with wild strawberry and raspberry, red-leaved blueberry and the interlacing drapery of the overshadowing firs, the forest closes in again.

But the Murvetz is merry this evening, welcoming a big party for dinner in a restaurant full of mounted boars' heads and scarlet peasant rugs. Logs are piled high round the huge hearth, but there is no need to light them yet; tonight, *raki* will warm everyone. The women are in sequinned jeans and thick make-up, the men hustling in leather jackets. Everyone is smoking. The occasion is plainly a celebration: probably the birthday of the small, tow-haired boy of five or six who is heaved on to the table, among the cruets and the glasses, with his gold cardboard crown and his plastic sword, to laughter and applause.

As his elders settle to their white-cheese salads, their *satch* of grilled chicken and Rhodopean potato pies, he runs from one end of the restaurant to the other. To and fro, back and forth. No one rebukes him. He moves with extraordinary grace, on tiptoe, twirling round each obstacle with his sword raised, singing. But as the professional singers begin their act onstage he falls silent, stealing close, listening for the moment when he can start to dance in time with them. Pirouetting then, raising his arms to show his small, bare stomach and his dangling, precious belt, he dances by himself. He is so absorbed in the music that he knows nothing else.

Everyone indulges him. The *chanteuse*, in black boots and a black dress slashed to mid-thigh, smiles fondly down on him. Waiters swerve round him, and the bearded keyboard-player lets him plink the upper register as he passes, briefly as a bird. He eats nothing, though the dessert is sheep's yogurt piled up like ice cream and half-drowned in walnuts and honey. Food is unnecessary. He has music to sustain him.

As the evening wears on he dances with his aunt, whose absurdly high heels mean she must bend down to take his fully outstretched arms; and with his mother, who picks him up to let him sway slowly to and fro with her. Pressed to her, in ecstasy, he buries his hands and his beaming face in her long blonde perfumed hair. Tenderly, once or twice, he kisses her. The *chanteuse* sings, in English, 'One Moment in Time'.

All around this small focus of sound and light, the forest sleeps. For mile upon mile, nothing stirs but the soft night wind in the high firs and the singing mountain streams. Tomorrow he will be there again, sitting by his father's van at the bend in the road to see if he can sell little plastic cups of blackberries, or potatoes packed in sacks as large as himself.

But tonight he is here, surrounded by wreaths of smoke and smiles, lifted up to the table again with his slipping-down trousers and his plastic sword, arrayed like a prince.

*

Konon, a Greek historian, declared that young Orpheus did not sing alone at Oeagros's court. He practised with other musicians in the palace, Macedonians as well as Thracians, 'and since they are a music-loving people, that made him very popular'. Nicomedes in his book *On Orpheus* – a lost biography, perhaps – mentioned the playing of a stringed phoinix at banquets given by Thracian princes, as though that was Orpheus's natural setting. But the music Xenophon heard at a Thracian banquet around 400 BC was mostly martial stuff: 'tunes on the horns used for signalling, flageolet notes on trumpets made of raw ox-hides', and high, light leaping to flutes by young men in armour, brandishing their knives. The banquet was more memorable for the diplomatic gifts that were exchanged, including a fine white horse, led whinnying and dancing to the table, and a slave.

Orpheus never seemed to belong there. Yet most traditions made him Thracian; and not merely that, but the king's heir, anticipated as the next ruler of his country. A fragment of Pindar called him 'Orpheus of the golden sword', an epithet also used of Apollo, whatever it meant. Most Thracians fought from their stirrupless horses with javelins and spears; but curved swords like scimitars were given as presents and buried with them, the hilts chased with gold and silver mined in the hills. Perhaps such a sword belonged to Orpheus; perhaps he knew how to use it. But his whole persona suggested otherwise. Music alone was his weapon and his defence. The real Orpheus, say some Bulgarian historians, was a Thracian king who tried to make his warring peoples live together in peace, and was killed when he failed.

He was not called a king again until the late Middle Ages. In the fourteenth and fifteenth centuries he became Sir Orpheus, riding through the greenwood with his retinue. This Orpheus was a young prince in ermine and silk, with a crown on his head. His descent from Apollo and Calliope ensured that he was 'gentill', or noble, and 'full of liberalite'. Ten thousand knights rode at his command; palaces, castles and wide estates belonged to him. Or he became Sir Orfeo, a creation with roots in Breton lays and Irish stories, who ruled in 'Traciens': not Thrace, but Winchester, in the steps of King Arthur. Little obviously linked him to the Orpheus of Plato, Philostratus, Ovid and Virgil. He was a knight of chivalry, armed and caparisoned to spend his days in thick-boughed, hound-belling woods, overcoming trials and tests to rescue his Beloved. But in one respect his character was unchanged. Though he hunted and hawked, his favourite occupation was to sing to the harp, which he had taught himself to play:

> He lerned so, there nothing was
> A better harpour in no plas.

That music — self-taught, mother-taught, breathed in from the winds and the gods — made up the whole track of his life, and love, and death.

Attic vase, fifth century BC

Second string: Trees

Orpheus was called the first poet, of whom all poets since are echoes or incarnations; yet no poetry definitely survives from him. Other people invented the dithyramb, the hymn, choruses and love songs. He was called the first musician, and the Emperor Nero explicitly dressed as him when he performed, laurel wreath askew and a pleated robe tight across his paunch; yet diatonic harmony and notes were invented by Phrygians, music itself by Zethus and Amphion, and the primitive lyre by Sicilians. Many, including Pindar, thought Orpheus was the first to compose chants for the lyre, the 'Father of Songs'. But no melodies or tunes were called his or described, except as a form of enchantment.

He was known familiarly as the *theologos*, the first singer of things divine, and was depicted sometimes with a basket of scrolls beside him, the hymns and prophecies he had been the first to write down. According to Athenagoras, Orpheus was 'the original inventor of the gods' names, and recounted their births and said what they have all done . . . and he is generally followed by Homer, especially about the gods.' His voice and name, from the dimmest reaches of antiquity, could lend authority to any philosophy or religion that came after him, including Christianity. Indeed, it was thought necessary, whether he had ever lived or not.

Among the works attributed to him were a treatise on astrology, another on plants (he was the first to write on botany, said Pliny the Elder), rules for initiations, calendars for crop-growing, a book called *Krater*, or *The Mixing-Bowl* (either about the oracular tripod of Apollo, or the making of dreams), books on temple-building, myth-making, the creation of the cosmos and – most certainly – the names of the gods. He wrote books with teasing, cryptic titles: *The Ball*, about the Earth, *The Robe*, on Nature, *The Net*, about the human body. And almost every one has vanished.

What remains? Only 'his own' mystical-magical account of the voyage of the Argonauts; eighty-seven hymns to the gods that were popularly, but tenuously, ascribed to him; and his *Lithica*, an 800-line poem on the magic properties of stones. Scattered fragments of his *Sacred Discourse in 24 Rhapsodies*, otherwise known as the *Rhapsodic Theogony* or the *Song of Creation*, turned up in the Derveni Papyrus that was found near Thessaloniki in 1962, and anciently in works by other people.

The *Argonautica* is late, probably from the fourth century AD. The hymns may be one or two centuries earlier, preserved in the cult book of a sect from Asia Minor; they are formulaic and mediocre, but flashes of his deeply secret originals were presumed to survive in them. The Derveni Papyrus, a commentary on his writings, seems to date from the fourth century BC and is the oldest manuscript yet found in Europe; the *Lithica*, with its gazetteer of twenty stones for healing and safety, against scorpions and hailstones, may be as early as the fifth century BC or eight centuries younger. What it owed to Orpheus, if anything, is lost in mist and speculation. Since his was the only name firmly attached to these works, they became part of his biography. In the catalogue of the London Library, and on the Internet, he is still their author. There is no one else.

Both Homer and Heraclitus may have borrowed from texts that 'Orpheus' wrote. But even in ancient times his poems were ascribed to Onomacritus, who either edited or forged them in Athens in the sixth century BC; his *Rhapsodic Theogony* was credited to Cercops the Pythagorean, and several others; while *The Robe* and *The Net* were said to be by Zopyrus of Heraclea or possibly by Pythagoras himself. Pausanias doubted that Orpheus really wrote his hymns – though there were some, in the keeping of certain priests at Athens, which he thought were probably genuine. Orpheus's name, everyone knew, was used with abandon; or perhaps he was simply given credit for any semi-divine inspiration, falling from Aether through the nerves to the pen, as Rilke felt him that February morning.

Within those writings, certain epithets seemed favourites with him. Rivers were always 'silver' and 'loud-roaring'. The motions of the universe, apparently so slow and stately, to him were 'flying', 'darting', 'rushing', the fastest words he could find, as if he had soared there himself 'like an eagle or a wind', and knew. Earth-life was 'weary', man's daily trudge, compared with the 'unwearying' gods. (Apollo in particular was *okueris*, quick-speaking, as he snapped out a father's commands.) Men were 'fleeting' and 'frail', moving over the earth in tribes like leaves, or flies, or sand. Winds were 'life-giving', feet 'swift' or running on tiptoe, and fruit more beautiful when it was green and forming. Nature was always generative and hectic, never still. Objects were never passive, always alive. He revelled in the soul and light of things. What he saw was what he sang.

He wrote, it was said, in the Pelasgian alphabet that predated the Phoenician, though no originals remained and no one was sure. 'Thracian tablets' held his spells, said Euripides, incised with his own hand, and other tablets of the great *theologos* lay on Mount Haimon somewhere. At Gela six writing-stones, covered with the proto-Cyrillic letters he was also said to have invented, were unearthed not long ago at the top of his mountain. But the truly wise knew he had not committed anything to paper, wax or stone. Plato, who was initiated in the Eleusinian Mysteries – related to those of Orpheus, but not the same – scattered this scrap and that, 'as Orpheus says', all through his *Dialogues*. As a child of the gods, he said, slightly tongue-in-cheek, Orpheus should have known what he was talking about. That was why he was worth quoting. But Plato also referred to him as a teacher of subversion, a prophet, one of the few – like Socrates – who was versed in *hieroi logoi*, sacred stories, and dared to disseminate them. 'Someone who does that', he added, 'has to be careful.' Orpheus risked attack, and would have been wise to disguise his teachings as something else. In fact, Plato thought, they ought still to be concealed in silence, 'because they are indicative of mystic conceptions, [and are] not fit for young men to hear'.

He wrote as one who knew. Olympiodorus said Plato imitated Orpheus's teachings 'in every respect', despite his general doubts about the usefulness of poets. Proclus too, in his fifth-century AD *Commentaries* on Plato, found the philosopher and the poet agreeing on almost everything. Plato certainly wrote as if he had felt his own cloak tugged, that music-breath in his own ear, at the corner of the *agora* in Athens where steps lead up through dusty oleanders to the temple of Zeus. He seemed to believe, with Proclus, that all Greek theology flowed from Orpheus's mystic symbols and suggestions. But Orpheus never came to the city, or persuaded – as Socrates had – 'the best young men' to abandon friends and family and follow him for their own improvement. The public square was always foreign to him. His school was not in any building, though the boys sitting now on the temple steps, smoking and listening to their iPods, may jiggle with the sense of him, and he slides through shaded doorways on the waves of balalaika music kicked up from passing cars. The forest was always his place, or among the rocks; in secret, and most often in the dark.

He was traditionally linked first to the worship of Dionysus, the son of Zeus and Semele, Mother-Earth. Zeus so terrified Semele with his thunder and lightning that she gave birth prematurely and died. For a few years the child Dionysus was brought up on Mount Ida in Crete, but then Zeus's jealous wife ordered him to be torn in pieces by the Titans, a race of earth-born giants. In their 'fatal insolence', as Orpheus put it, they distracted the child with toys, killed him, sliced him into seven pieces, boiled and tasted him. The pieces they dispersed. Zeus, inconsolable, shattered the Titans with lightning and, from their ashes, created a new race of men made partly of that blaze from Heaven, partly of Earth: ashes and fire. Dionysus, scattered through the world, represented the lightning in them. He was also the world-soul, torn apart and flung into the animal life of earth. But his career was far from over.

His heart was rescued from the carnage. When the rest of his body was dispersed, it remained, beating and undivided. Zeus stitched the heart with golden pins into his own shining, muscled thigh, where it regenerated. The boy was born again, nursed by satyrs and nymphs in secret in a cave on Mount Nysa in Arabia: 'twice-born', as Orpheus called him, called back from death into life. He was a languid, pretty young man, not unlike Apollo, his golden hair knotted with cooling ivy and honeysuckle or crimped tight in a headband to help his hangovers. He was reported in purple coats, a golden crown and shoes with golden straps; his scheming eyes were so alight with love-fire that no woman was safe with him. He kept a ménage of them, faithfully following his tipsy, priapic progress even as far as India, 'over the wine-coloured sea'. But he became, under pressure and inspiration, a writhing snake and a raging bull, symbols of eternity and the sacred force of life.

Thrace was the centre of his cult, which had spread there from Asia Minor and Crete. Oeagros, Orpheus's putative father, was sometimes said to have been a master of the rites, learning them from his own father (who had learned them directly from the god) and teaching his teenage son after him. But Apollodorus, Lactantius, Diodorus and Herodotus, to name a few, thought at least some elements of these Mysteries had been introduced by Orpheus himself.

Dionysus in Thrace was worshipped as *Bassareus*, the cunning fox god, as well as the god of wine and life. To be his priest involved wearing the fox-skin cap and *bassarai*, long fox-skin robes lined and fringed with white wool; to leap and stamp in the dark, drink deep, cry out prophecies, in order to achieve union with Dionysus himself. The shaman became the god and the worshippers followed, swept up in his *orgia* or 'burstings-forth'. 'Then everyone's bonds sprang loose,' as Orpheus described it. In transformation, the grape-followers of Dionysus were deliriously smashed into wine.

The mystical side of this was understood later by Rumi, the great poet of Sufism:

> The grapes of my body can only become wine
> After the winemaker tramples me.
> I surrender my spirit like grapes to his trampling
> So my inmost heart can blaze and dance with joy.

The communion on the Thracian mountains was cruder and bloodier. After a few gulps from the goblet, young Orpheus would begin to feel it: the beat, beat, beat of life thumped out on goat-skin drums, crashed out on cymbals. 'Drum-beating, brass-sounding' life – Dionysian life – burst through the earth, split the buds, blazed in the grass. It shocked like shrill tambourines, shaking down as rain through leaves or as foaming cataracts through the rocks. Piping on the double pipes, it filled the trees with wild, howling songs. Orpheus's heart pounded with that same raw creation music, whirling beat after beat. His elegant lyre would have been drowned out. With his waving, phallic thyrsus, made from a giant fennel-stalk or cut from green ash-boughs, he would try to direct the worshippers. But this was less dancing than wild, free running, so crazed (as Euripides described it in *The Bacchae*) that the whole mount - ain seemed to be on the move, and he as a long-legged boy among them:

> hurling
> my throat to the dewy air of heaven,
> like a fawn playing in the green
> pleasures of a meadow
> when it has escaped the terrifying
>   hunt, beyond the watchers,
>   over the well-woven nets;
>   . . . and with gales of swift
>   running it bounds over the plain
>   by the river, rejoicing . . .

He was the fawn running and the fox leaping, both of them soft-footed Dionysus, the god of the waking and greening earth.

At the climax came the *sparagmos*, the tearing-in-pieces. It mimicked the fate of Dionysus and also what happened to shamans of Thrace, when they died to the body and were reborn. The dancers fell to the ground, as if dead themselves. Bullocks and goats were ripped apart, their flesh chewed raw, warm blood forced down, while the mad god-greeting '*Evoi! Evoi!*' rang among the rocks. The main orgiastic rites took place in midwinter; blood spattered the snow. In this savage sacrament the worshippers took on the nature of the torn, trembling, 'blessed and leaping' god. Men roared like bulls, women wore bull-horns. (Women especially were maddened by the god's proximity, turned into Maenads with wild, rank hair whipping across their eyes.) The god was hymned in loud, fast choral dithyrambs, underpinned by drums, impossible to lead off unless you were intoxicated. Drunk, then, Orpheus sang them out, loudest and first.

Regularly he would climb to the oracle of Dionysus on a

high peak of the Rhodopes, crunching through the incessant snow and the silent, snow-laden trees. Cold amulets, sacred to the god, hung on the lower branches. He would climb in the looming dusk, crowned with black-berried ivy and using his thyrsus as a staff, to the places of night-gatherings, Kithaeron, Helicon and Pangaion, where perhaps he had first seen daylight. They would be lit now by pine-pitch or oak-splint torches, flowing and flaring among the familiar rocks, and by the soft background glow of the god's presence there. By day, he rode; priests of Dionysus had the pick of the Thracian horses, as Rhesus (also a shaman-prince of Thrace) did in Homer's *Iliad*: 'bigger and lovelier than any, whiter than snow, running like the wind', or like the steeds of the sun god across the sky.

Clement of Alexandria, master of the school in that city around AD 205, a pagan convert to Christianity still half-fascinated by what he had abandoned, revealed fragments of the rites. Their symbol was a consecrated serpent, he wrote, the world-spirit who was also Dionysus, pictured sometimes twining around the tree where Orpheus sang. And speaking of snakes, the Maenads plaited their hair with them, or with snaking ivy-roots, as barbarians would. Euripides, seething with prurient curiosity, gave glimpses six centuries earlier: he mentioned 'crowned goblets' brimming with wine, standing in a clearing, and special seats from which the shamans, by daylight, observed the flight of birds. The wax or wooden phallus of the god was carried around and worshipped. Little else was revealed to the uninitiated. Lips and eyes were sealed. It was assumed a lot of sex went on, on holy fawn-skins strewn on the ground. Maenads danced ecstatically with snakes, draping them across their breasts or between their naked thighs. Young mothers, posing as Dionysus's own nurses or the fecund, nurturing Earth, suckled fawns and wolf-cubs; Orpheus too, perhaps, was allowed the gorged teat to taste their sweet, sticky flow. 'Let's leave him there,' concluded Clement, 'with the satyrs, and the frenzied rabble, and the rest of the demon crew' – pausing only to ram a crown of ivy on his lolling, drunken head.

Yet it was always difficult to consign him to that place. Apollo was already mooted as his father; his lyre proclaimed him a disciple, and he was possibly already Apollo's priest in private. His affinity with alphabets and metre, as well as his instinctive calm, suggested Apollonian organisation in his character: 'the immeasurable principle of order', as his hymns called it. Dionysus-worship could not have suited him. To eat life, in the form of quivering flesh and blood that still flowed hot, would have sickened him. The life of beast and bird and even grass-blade was also his own, a music he shared. Horror must at last have sent him stumbling away, out of the rampaging firelight into the dark, his fur robes slick with sweat and the wine-breath sour in his mouth, to retch among the rocks of Helicon and Kithaeron until the dawn came, smeared with red.

Nonetheless, he stayed. In the sixth century BC, when he became famous, Dionysus and Apollo were not at odds. In Orpheus's version of the story, Apollo had received from Zeus the fragments of the divine child and taken them to his own shrine on Parnassus. At Delphi, too, the oracle was protected by Apollo for half the year and by Dionysus for the other half. They worked together. Orpheus himself potentially bridged the divide: the son of a tattooed Thracian,

master of the cult of disorder, or the son of the divine, light-
bringing player of the lyre. As Jungian psychology later
analysed him, he was both the mouthpiece of forces beyond
himself and a voice of his own, individual and alone. He was
both possessed and free. Rilke, in a vision ten years before
Orpheus was with him, saw this double persona even among
the angels:

> Spaces of being, force-fields of ecstasy, storms
> of unchecked rapture, and suddenly separate
> *mirrors* – each drawing its own widespread
> streaming beauty back into its face –

The young Friedrich Nietzsche saw Orpheus's dilemma
differently. In 1872 he encountered him, or one like him, 'in
Dionysian drunkenness and mystical self-abnegation', alone at
the edge of the revelling choruses, sinking to the ground. This
should have been a moment of rapture. Instead, it was despair.
As a Dionysus-worshipper, Orpheus had become the god. As
a devotee of Apollo, he could only paint the god, sing him or
dream him from afar. Amid the wildness of the crowd, he had
been one with all Nature; now, sobering up, he was on the
edge, cut off, and merely an observer. His exile from godhead
was made bearable only by the beauty he created in his separated state. In his loneliness lay the root of all the tragedies
ever written, and all the sad songs ever heard.

Theologians and philosophers also found echoes in him of
the Babylonian scriptures, the Chaldean sacred writings and the
Vedas of the Hindus. The theogonies were often close. The

ancient, secret teachings had been transmitted through Zoroaster and Hermes Trismegistus; they had probably infiltrated from India, via Asia Minor, to join up with Thracian shaman-teachings by the sixth century BC, when Orpheus appeared. The result was a set of doctrines, and a parade of gods, that seemed bafflingly complicated. Some also found it disagreeable. Isocrates said Orpheus related more unseemly stories about the gods than any other poet he knew: tales of castration, self-copulation, premature ejaculation, eating of children. (And fellatio, too, added Diogenes Laertius.) They were not meant literally. But there was perhaps no other way to tell the story of the world's beginnings, simply, memorably but covertly, in songs. The pure of heart and mind would understand.

All accounts of Orpheus's *Rhapsodic Theogony* disagreed with each other, and the original had vanished. It had probably been left in disconnected fragments, which various hands, at various times, had tried to put together. Proclus, who related snippets and scraps in his *Commentaries* on Plato, seemed the best source for it. For him, there was no doubt that Orpheus was real. Proclus taught courses on his books, and on what Iamblichus and Syrianus had to say about them. He also longed to write his own Orpheus commentary, but out of fear, or respect, for Syrianus he contented himself with making remarks in the margins of other peoples'. 'We don't accept the theories of Amelius and Theodorus,' he remarked, somewhat archly, at one point, 'but we shall stick with the theories of Plato and Orpheus.' Those were tricky enough, but, to him at least, they seemed true.

According to Proclus, Orpheus taught that the first cause was Undecaying Time, boldly giving it a name when most theologists did not dare. (Even Plato did not dare, said Proclus, but Orpheus 'gets his inspiration from a higher realm'.) Some might object, of course, that the first cause surely lay outside Time. But Orpheus would reply – Proclus said – that Time took the lead in all generation, one thing following another, and so naturally came first.

Time coupled with Ananke, or Compulsion, both twining like snakes in utter emptiness, though as yet there were no forms. From these sprang Aether and Chaos, the one binding and limiting, the other an infinite and bottomless chasm; and from the marriage of these came Being as a great Cosmic Egg, 'silver-shining' like mother-of-pearl. (Of course, Proclus added, the Olympian gods had not really called these things 'Time' or 'Aether' or 'Chaos' or 'Egg'; Orpheus had deliberately chosen names from 'the lowest levels of reality' in order to part-reveal, part-conceal.) The Egg began to move steadily, in a great circle. Then out of it burst Phanes, 'the Manifestor' and the first of the gods, ripping through Aether as he came 'in unexpected light'. With a roar of harmony, music came with him. He was both male and female, golden-winged and 'gloriously beautiful'. As C.G. Jung saw him in vision in September 1917, he was 'the smile of dawn, the resplendent day, the immortal present . . . hunger and satiation, love and lust, promise and fulfilment'. Orpheus gave him the heads of a bull, a ram, a serpent and a man, because he was the source of all forms. His name, in Greek, derived from *phanein*: blazing torches, shining stars.

Night came with him, sometimes as his sister, sometimes his daughter. She alone could see him, though his radiance filled all creation. He either mated with himself, or with her, and together they produced all phenomena: Heaven and Earth and Ocean, the blessed gods and the men they made, 'unfolded into the light'. All things were contained in them and they were in everything, supreme in subordinate, lower in higher. Ceaselessly, the same themes and patterns repeated. So Heaven was both aetherial and earthly; the stars were made of both Heaven and Earth; and man, too, had Heaven and Earth in him. Around him Nature was both finite and infinite, corruptible and everlasting, 'whirling on the still-standing tips of her toes': for in Orpheus's theology everything, from the atoms to the stars, moved in circles of reciprocal desire, and Love made everything dance.

His teachings, Proclus said, placed six generations of gods in charge of creation: Phanes, Night, Heaven, Kronos, Zeus and Dionysus. All these were one god in different aspects, steadily more manifest, endlessly creating and annihilating. Phanes, the first intelligible god, had the original idea of what creation should be. All forms were his thoughts, sent forth like swarms of bees to frame and fill the cosmos. But then Night prophesied to Zeus that he would usurp him; and Zeus swallowed him, with all his forms and ideas, to bring them into being again. Everything was contrived anew, sang Orpheus:

> the gleaming height of Aether and wide Heaven,
> splendid Earth, the foundations of the sea,
> mighty Ocean and Tartarus, darkest and deepest,
> rivers and seas in their immensity,
> all the immortal blessed gods and goddesses,
> all that has been born and will come to be . . .

'King' Zeus marshalled fiery particles into the mass of the sun, moved it aside to allow the shapes of matter to coagulate and form in the cooling air, scattered the surplus sparks over Heaven as fixed stars, and forged creation with his 'bright bolt' as blacksmiths used fire. (For Orpheus's pupils there was a deeper, secret meaning, to be revealed when they were ready.) Only human beings proved hard to manage. They contained not only the aether-lightning of Zeus, not only the scattered life-spark of Dionysus, but also the savagery of the Titans who had killed him. The burden of that original sin had to be overcome. The soul had to be cleansed by religious rites and punishments after death to earn immortality again. That hard road was Orpheus's teaching – and the teaching of all Christian churches long after him.

Some of these ideas had come from Egypt. Indeed, Diodorus thought most of them had. Orpheus was widely assumed to have studied in 'golden' Alexandria, eagerly rifling through the huge library to interpret hieroglyphs of soul-birds, all-seeing eyes, river-waves, ears of wheat. Outside, in the broiling heat that reddened and blistered his pale Thracian skin, he would have walked on the banks of the great river, observing the stagnant mud pools where creatures could be seen forming and half-forming out of the slime, as at the very beginning of the world. Gods had been spawned there, too: Zeus, Hermes, Apollo, Pan, rising out of the Nile when it was still elemental Ocean wrestling with elemental Earth. Or so the scholars told him.

According to his own *Argonautica*, he also went to 'Memphis and the holy towns of Apis' on the Nile. 'I brought forth the sacred tale at Memphis,' he said, presumably meaning his *Rhapsodic Theogony*, or *Song of Creation*, in all its hundreds of lines. And some supposed he travelled further. At Nysa in neighbouring Arabia a narrow glen of great beauty, rushing with water, led to the cave where reborn Dionysus had been brought up in secret. Again, Diodorus set the scene. Rocks of every colour – shellfish-purple, blue, red – towered above it, and evergreens and fruit trees overshadowed it. The birds here sang more sweetly, it was said, than anywhere else. Lying on the grassy banks ('the couches of the nymphs', as the guides called them), where the cave opened into the woods and the sun bathed him, Orpheus could imagine the tottering, dancing steps of the hidden child-god, his babbling and bright hair. He made songs of it. Here too, in the 'land of spices', where the markets were stacked with sweet, dusty bundles and the earth itself contained veins of perfume, he would have found the resins and aromatics that he later used to reinforce his prayers: red balsam, pitch pine, vanilla-scented storax, cassia and golden crocus, frankincense in white cubes. And myrrh, oily on his fingers, whose dreadful story Ovid made him sing: the warm, thick, golden tears of a girl who had loved her father and had been turned into a tree, her trunk splitting open in a red gash to drop his child into the grass.

In Egypt, Diodorus wrote, Orpheus became 'the foremost of the Greeks in theology, cult ceremonies, poetry and music'. He visited the temples of the Egyptians, craning his neck in huge pillared halls where the walls were embedded with jewels and painted with gold; he saw their shrines, hidden behind gold-embroidered curtains, where the laughing priest would half-reveal on a purple couch a sacred crocodile, a serpent or a cat. Outside the temples, crouching sphinxes proclaimed the obscurity of God. Music was played here on cross-flutes and single pipes, both instruments that were strange to him, said to be inventions of the sun god Osiris; Alexandria was full of the sound of pipes and harps, which even the humblest citizen knew how to play. In ceremonial processions he would have noted that the Singer walked first, playing a lyre with one curved, curious arm, while the Astrologer followed him.

Like Pythagoras later, Orpheus would have been circumcised before he was allowed to know the Egyptian Mysteries. Only the purified and passionless could approach them. They were contained in thirty-six hieroglyphic books of Thoth, or Hermes, the ibis-headed god, which were memorised by the Singer, the Astrologer and the other priests. Orpheus, too, was thought to have memorised them. Dissemination was not allowed. These things were to be wrapped in metaphors, enigmas and silence: lessons he learned so well for his own poems that many books were needed, such as Syrianus's now-lost two volumes *On the Theology of Orpheus*, to unravel the 'peculiarities' in them.

Those who thought Orpheus had borrowed from Egypt found plenty of suggestive evidence. He admitted bringing 'Egyptian laments, libations of Osiris', home with him. His firstborn of the gods, Phanes, sprang from a cosmic egg, as did Ra, the first of the Egyptian gods. Both were radiant, but invisible. Osiris seemed a model for his own Dionysus, 'Shining One', as he called him, in a fawn-skin cloak that represented the sky strewn with stars. Osiris, like Dionysus, introduced the vine and began the custom of wine-drinking, or sharing ecstatically in the boundless nature of the god. He too was killed, dismembered and gathered up again, his limbs fished up by the god Theut out of the Nile – though, unlike Dionysus, he did not come back to life.

Diodorus thought Orpheus had invented Dionysus by simply taking Osiris and making him Greek. But the cult of Dionysus was older than Orpheus was, by most accounts. If he borrowed, he also blended, recognising where gods were essentially the same. So Isis, the Egyptian moon goddess, was sometimes Thracian Artemis, bull-horned in her crescent days, and sometimes his own Demeter, the wheat goddess, walking in her holy fields. All three governed the growth of things. The discovery by Isis of wheat and barley had also made flesh-eating unnecessary; and it was perhaps in Egypt, with its strange diet of flatbread, lentils and lily tubers, that Orpheus turned to an ascetic and vegetarian life. Rumi later described Egyptian bread as 'stale the next day': like knowledge, hymnody, cosmology, all crammed in by the eager young Thracian, it had to be eaten fresh.

Within the temples, robed in white linen and pledged to silence, he heard of a kingdom of the dead and the journey of souls, towards immortality, in a reed boat on a river; of chambers, throne rooms and balance-scales in a lower world; of punishments for wrongdoers and fields of joy for the righteous; of the wheel of birth, death and rebirth. Outside, he noticed long, shallow boats crossing the Nile with the coffins of the dead. A silent boatman was in charge of them, poling his craft across the turbid water. On the other side lay meadows of extraordinary lushness, thick with reeds and rose-coloured lotuses that made a man forget the world. Orpheus began, Diodorus said, to make up adventure stories there. Herodotus noted that the Thracians placed coins and amulets on their dead to pay ferry-charges to the Underworld, and thought they had picked up that habit from the Egyptians. He did not ask how. In one Thracian grave of the eighth to sixth century BC a small green scarab beetle, the Egyptian symbol of the reborn and rising sun, appeared on a necklace that was buried with the dead, as Orpheus might also have suggested.

His prayers, too, acquired a foreign cast. His name for the ineffable first principle was 'the thrice-unknown darkness', an Egyptian formula. The sun became several gods, receding into eternity. His own philosophy came to centre on the fates of the pure and the impure soul. And his lasting fame was linked to an Underworld that he may have seen, at first, as the Egyptians drew and painted it, or with an Egyptian guide beside him.

However his ideas had originated, they were then made many times more complicated. As the putative founder of all Greek theology and philosophy, Orpheus needed not merely songs and stories, but a system. That system, said the Pythagoreans, was based on number. Pythagoras himself had written (said Iamblichus) that when he was initiated in the Thracian Mysteries, 'the initiating priest shared with me what Orpheus son of Calliope said, having learned it from his mother, on Mount Pangaion: *Number is the eternal and provident principle of heaven and earth and what is between, and the source of the continuing existence of divine persons, gods and spirits.*'

No number theogonies, or bits of celestial geometry, were mentioned in any fragment of Orpheus that survives. His love of circles seemed active and elemental; he never measured or divided them, simply danced them, as a Dervish or a Sufi would. But Pythagoreans felt they had to make a mathematician of him, as well as an astronomer and an astrologer. Iamblichus insisted that Pythagoras 'emulated Orpheus's interpretation [of the gods] in all respects': even setting up, instead of statues, glowing bronze dodecahedrons, 'the sphere of the all'.

Believing this, the Neoplatonists taught that Orpheus had devised a system that expressed the perfect structure of the universe. Beyond the visible world, his creation contained super-sensible, intellectual and intelligible realms, the last open only to the serenest minds, where Phanes flashed like summer lightning. The planets floated in shining, egg-like envelopes called 'wholenesses', the universe in little. In each of these swarmed all the gods, from Zeus to Poseidon, coloured with that planet's character and light. Gods were everywhere; Theophilus said that Orpheus believed in 365 of them. They were arranged in triads, then in dodecads, to reflect their creative, preserving or regenerative power. The fundamental unit of creation was the monad or atom, and even the least of these reflected every other. In particular, since man was the microcosm of the universe, this whole elaborate architecture and all these potential powers were also mirrored in him.

Few minds could claim to understand all this. Plato, of course, had followed it completely, but he had chosen to reveal it only in careful asides, which Proclus then had to explain. Most people left it well alone. And in the end the details scarcely mattered, for Orpheus's legions of gods were essentially principles or aspects of one unutterable power. To that power, couched in darkness and silence, all the gods were united like rays to a source or like tree-roots, as Orpheus saw them, growing inwards. At the still centre, in a reverse of the process of creation, all opposites were resolved and all distinctions lost. Plato kept hold of an Orpheus-scrap, from one of his hymns to Zeus, and used it like a mantra, repeating it often to bring to mind that One in which all became the same:

> fire and water,
> Earth and Aether,
> night and day.

Proclus offered another fragment: rest and motion were one, the Same and the Other were one, 'and all were undivided in the darkling mist, as Orpheus says.'

Again, the dark. Orpheus approached it with such devotion that perhaps this was the origin of his mysterious name: not *eu-phonos*, beautiful-voiced, but *orphe*, darkness. Darkness as the womb of light. He invoked it with the fervour of a scientist for dark matter, the unseen side of things. The dark was his place, from which he had come and into which he compulsively journeyed; Night was his time, when he taught, danced and prayed:

> O Nurse supreme of all the powers divine,
> Immortal Night!

'Swift Night', he sang, possessed 'the truth of the gods'. She alone had seen Phanes, the firstborn, bull-headed and golden-winged, roaring out the energy of first life progressing into first forms, with the first light glittering from his skin. She alone, by sheer contrast, made light appear. In both the upper and the lower worlds, Light manifested life until Night ruled again. All creation, he sang – Aether, wide Heaven, the Earth, the sea and the constellations – was produced from Night, the Mother of Dreams, 'glistening with stars'. And all that man created, too, came from the night that lay within him.

Or perhaps his name had another, related source. It might mean *orphanos*, an orphan, separated from Phanes, longing for light, as all things in his cosmology longed for their opposites. His singing joined him again to the 'radiant young sapling' from which everything had formed and to which all things returned. His teachings, said his disciple Musaeus, had one simple theme: 'Everything comes into being from the One and is resolved into the One again.'

*

The lyre, or cithara, is central. He lifts it down now or swings it from his shoulder on its wide gold strap, preparing to play. The whole instrument buzzes, thrums, is already alive. It is light, or familiarity makes it so. A second strap slips over his left wrist to hold it steady. From a long red cord attached to the base hangs the plectrum, a small carved quill of ivory, swinging slightly. But he will not use it yet.

Tuning must come first. Each recital begins with a careful tightening of the pegs on the cross-bar, twisting them in their socket of red threads as each string is plucked and tested. He uses his thumb for this, softer and subtler than the plectrum, his head bent to the vibrating string and his lips slightly open, breathing quickly, as over the body of a lover.

The sound he is searching for is bright, high and dry, 'tense-

ness' as opposed to 'slackness': the exact tone, he will tell
you, of his own soul and the Aether from which his soul has
come. His scales are pitched in the Dorian enharmonic mode,
in which the two inner notes of the tetrachord are quarter-
tones or less: *pyknon*, or 'condensations', to the Greeks. As he
plucks the notes of the Dorian scale – D below middle C, E,
E raised a quarter-tone, F, A, B, B raised a quarter-tone, middle
C – the effect is almost Indian. You might well believe he has
travelled towards you from the dry plains of the subcontinent,
rather than the mountains of Thrace. Gurus would meditate
to this; or, as he would say, music in this mode will return
the soul to the Aether while it lasts. It makes people solemn
and calm, hushed to quiet. But tuning of the proper delicacy
and sobriety is almost impossible to achieve. The watery realms
of incarnation constantly slacken the strings, pulling them out
of tune as the soul is pulled by the restlessness and weight of
the body. There is nothing he can do except tune and retune,
pluck and listen, until he strikes that note of perfection; until
he can override the earth-tones, and relax into a smile.

His lyre has seven strings. You may see them as the seven
spheres through which he will lead souls to Heaven, the seven
stars of his Roman portraits; or as Christian doctrines, virtues,
sacraments. They can be the rainbow's seven colours, splitting out of white light, as silence produces the seven notes of
the scale. But his own philosophy also gives them a secret
meaning. 'At the sixth note,' he wrote once, 'bring to a close
the order of the song.' Plato quotes that remark in the *Philebus*
without explaining what he means, and Orpheus will not tell
you now, no matter how much you press him. He sings such
things only 'for those with insight'; you should not need to

ask. Six notes symbolise his six generations of the creating gods, from Phanes to Dionysus. Beyond the sixth note lies the dissolution of all created things.

As he holds the lyre, clasped to his left side and tilted away from him, the deepest sound belongs to the string that lies closest to his body. He calls it *hypate*. According to Diodorus, Orpheus himself added this string to the lyre. It is Saturn's note, perhaps a Thracian one, distant, strange. He deliberately leaves it a little slack, to resonate slower with a dark, contrasting sound. The highest note, *nete*, his favourite, comes from the furthest string and is the moon's note, white-shining like her. As he sweeps the plectrum across the strings, emphatically outwards and away from him – still testing, getting it right – his music thrills higher. *Hypate* also signifies winter, bruised light and buried life; *nete* the bright and cricket-shrilling summer. The strings between hold the tones of autumn and spring. When Apollo plays these, he brings the seasons into being. All revolves round *mese*, the middle string, as creation in Orpheus's philosophy revolves around Love.

Yet Neoplatonists insist that the notes are less important than the spaces that lie between them. Those harmonic intervals express the exact mathematical structure of the universe: the ratio, as Simplicius wrote, 'between the sun and moon, Venus and Mercury, and the other stars'. Orpheus himself is said to have discovered these, perhaps on a journey to the depths of the sky. The same ratio also exists within himself, and the beauty and purpose of music is to link them, binding the harmonies of heavenly spheres and the human soul; as Plato said in the *Phaedo*, 'tuning the soul-circuits in us'. That is the deepest reason why Orpheus sings, and why he plays.

He turns the last peg, plucks the last string, and pauses. He is ready now. In the painting Philostratus saw in Naples, he was just like this:

> his left foot steady on the ground supports the cithara which rests upon his thigh; his right foot, in its sandal, marks the time by beating the ground. His right hand firmly grasps the plectrum, giving close heed to the notes with the elbow extended and the wrist bent inward, while the left with straight fingers strikes the strings.

The cithara is bigger, boxier and made for the stage, but even this he does not play showily. His style – the proper ancient style, as Plutarch described it in his *Moralia* – is confined to a few notes, played 'with simplicity and grandeur'. His singing is the same, and it is this that will bewitch you: the purity and beauty of his voice. To modern ears the tone is high, but to the Greeks this was perfection: *ligyros*, sweet and clear, a word also applied to nightingales, cicadas, the wind, and the lyre itself. He throws his head back to sing, his spine straight, projecting as clearly and as far as he can. In this too he imitates the birds, noting how far their song carries in the stillness of the fields. Before the *Argo* voyage he sang in a centaur's cave, sending his notes as far as the valley floor and to the summit of Mount Pelion, where the oaks began to stir. The centaur clapped wildly, and drummed his iron-shod hooves on the ground.

There are no tricks here. Each note is exactly pitched and detached. No sliding or eliding, no sudden switching of harmonies, no odd rhythms; just one stately melodic line, in a rhythm of heroic hexameters. This, people say, is the tempo of the gods. Orpheus will tell you that Zeus handed down the quadratic hexameter of twenty-four measures, the rhythm of creation, to Apollo, who handed it to him. Like a sceptre it passed from god to god and into his own merely human fingers, trembling with light and power. That is why his masterpiece, the *Song of Creation*, is in twenty-four rhapsodies. It re-enacts the making of the world through the musical vibrations that still ring in everything, from stone, to water, to wood, to flesh.

Yet there is nothing grand or elaborate in it. Song and accompaniment always match each other, simplicity itself. All his songs are hymns, of praise or supplication; in the age of deep myth in which he lives, there is nothing else. Plato says there must be divine madness in them. In a way, Orpheus agrees: in the *Argonautica* he sings of inspiration as a ravaging gadfly, a goad, a sting, possessing his body for a while and then abandoning it, like something dead, to seek the sky. Apollo sends it; Calliope supplies the words, as if he is still a small child embraced and held close to the lyre. Yet for all this parental pushing, his songs suggest the unforced joy of a shepherd boy singing, or the raptness of a priest at prayer. He reinforces his music by dancing, but it is nothing wild: just swaying or stepping on the spot on tiptoe, forwards, backwards, to the side, because Apollo when he plays is a dancer, and this is how, in the cosmos, the planets move around the sun.

Rilke, hearing this singing close on that February morning, remarks that it seems like breathing. Orpheus takes in space, husbands it in his innermost heart, then gives it back as 'an invisible poem' of his own experience. Space expands with his song, with his breath. This is singing as being: *Gesang ist Dasein*, just an effortless wafting, or a wind barely felt. He sings of the visible world he has plundered, or of the invisible world Death sees: what Rilke, at his dictation, calls 'the other side of the air'. In either mode the simplicity works like a mantra, soothing the heart and stirring the soul: kindling it so deeply that, like a butterfly that beats against the window, soft blue wings whirring faintly, it longs to leave.

Easy for a god, Rilke writes. *Ein Gott vermags*. So easy that it needs not even will or desire, just a heart tuned and open to that inner song of infinite space. ('When', he asks him, 'will you pour the earth and the stars into *us*?') Yet – though Rilke cannot help thinking of him this way, cannot resist calling him 'du', as friend, god, Master – this is not a god who sings. Only a semi-god, a poet like him, who at the end coughs or smiles or eases his throat with water, replacing the glass on the table with a quiet intentness, while spirit sleeps again in the dampened strings.

One of 'his' books was called *The Lyre*. Since all was symbolism with him, and nothing plain, it was about the ascent of souls. No trace of it survives, and no other clue was offered as to how his music worked, or what it meant. That was left to others. To young Marsilio Ficino, for example, sitting in a room at the Careggi Academy in Florence, his head, too, bent intently over the strings. Fifteenth-century sunlight filtered through the glass; marble and red roof-tiles clustered beyond it. He wore a velvet bonnet and a long, floppy-sleeved Polish shirt – his Orpheus clothes, as he thought of them – for to himself and his friends he seemed to be Orpheus back on the earth again, in Florence in 1468. The soul of the Thracian singer had migrated, possibly through Homer, Ennius and Pythagoras, into him.

Ficino was steeped in 'our Plato', now restored to grace

in Italy and studied by him, in pride of place, at the Academy that he and Cosimo de Medici had just founded together. He aimed to show that Plato and Christianity could be reconciled, despite the doubters. He was equipped too with Orpheus's hymns, brought to Florence thirty years before, newly discovered in a bundle of vellum rolls near the temple of Demeter at Pergamum, in Asia Minor. These hymns, with their disturbing pagan cadences, he had translated into Latin but not published, concerned as a Christian that vulgar readers might miss the truth in them and pick out the profanity; worried, too, as Orpheus would have been, about revealing secret things.

Instead Ficino kept them for his own use. He sang them for hours on end, *ritu Orphico*, to his own lyre. It was an exact reconstruction, with a picture of 'the divine prophet' painted on the shell. He found that the step-by-step quarter-tones relaxed him and stopped him, in his words, 'becoming unstrung'. They also made a sort of prayer that seemed unusually effective. A begging note to Cosimo, for example, enclosing Ficino's translation of Orpheus's 'Hymn to Heaven' (*uranos* deftly altered to *cosmos* throughout), brought money at once. Sometimes, when he had finished a letter or a page of a book, he would jump up, seize the lyre, find himself rising up on tiptoe, and sing 'with incredible sweetness' music never heard before. Some of his contemporaries insisted that Orpheus declaimed in sung speech and played the *lira da braccio* with a bow, in the modern style. Ficino knew better. Orpheus would have performed exactly as he did. His friends imagined that the trees danced then, completing the effect, and the birds flew down to him.

Yet such a mood might have been too convivial, too full of joy. Ficino found melancholy necessary, a gloomy emptiness ready to be filled with the *furor divinus*, the wind-breath of inspired song. This flowed through space from God, mingling in a subtle vapour inside him that came from his own heart. It all depended, too, on the middle part of the brain:

> When this part of the brain is not in tune, it does not respond
> at all to the universal harmony. On the other hand, when it
> is in tune, it is wonderfully moved by the universal harmony,
> as though by something totally similar.

This harmony, Ficino knew, was God himself. He had learned this from Orpheus very young. It was not quite Christian doctrine, but he did not abjure it. Orpheus's music, he noted, was a sort of natural magic, and that magic too was an act of love, as iron was irresistibly drawn to the magnet, or flowers to the light. It was a turning of crea-ture to Creator that completed, in a circle or a mirror, creation itself. And it was also the means for his soul to go back to the Heaven it had once known. The effect of his divine music, ringing from the Careggi Academy past the neat, trembling bay trees and across the marble floors, was to lead his listeners note by note towards God, and towards Love.

Orpheus taught all this. He goes on teaching it wherever he is heard. Without the lyre, and the love the lyre expresses, souls cannot return. With the lyre, sweeping upwards from dark *hypate* to shining *nete*, he plays the scale of the soul's ascending, as well as – in Macrobius's words – 'a memory of the music which it knew in the sky'.

And it is the heart he plays: the patient receptacle of his soul-song, its sound-box, strings and shell.

*

Shakespeare would have understood. He spoke of Orpheus's own sinews stringing his lyre, as the spider its web. And George Herbert too, writing a little later, played on that image. He made the heart a resonating sound-box, a taut wired instrument which, like his lute, would 'struggle' and 'twist' to sing. He found other metaphors for it: a trussed pack like a pedlar's, to be unlaced only by God; a writing box, containing ink and the folded record of his sins; a nest of drawers within boxes within chests within cupboards, mitred and locked against affliction; a bowl of cream. But he returned most often to the heart as lute, the instrument he knew. He tried to make a 'kind of tune' on it, the best he could manage, to the God he loved and served. And sometimes, suddenly – unexpectedly – that tune would become a faltering hymn of praise:

> Church bells beyond the stars heard, the soul's blood,
> The land of spices, something understood.

Rilke, too, when his praising was done at Orpheus's pushing, wrote that his heart was so convalescent, 'since it slipped from the hand of that god who shook it so strenuously', that he dared not inspect it. He was played out, and even breathing was now a perilous act.

But Orpheus sang, careless of danger. An Attic vase of the fifth century BC draws the ancient scene for us: the poet throwing his head back, 'singing the heart', and four Thracians listening. They may be shepherds or hunters; no one knows.

They have stopped on a journey through the mountains, in their long travelling mantles and lynx-skin caps, and rest on their spears or staves as men may do who have come across some extraordinary wild creature. One stands close enough to touch him, hand arrogantly on hip as if to say, 'Show me.' Another stands wrapped defensively in his cloak, shoulders hunched and feet turned away, ready to run or resist. A third listens with his eyes closed, in rapture.

Orpheus on this vase has been made Greek, to show him as a civilised man among the savages of Thrace. His cloak has the same decorated border as theirs, but he wears it Greek-fashion, simply draped from the waist. He has nothing on his torso and a wreath around his hair; his feet, like the travellers', are bare. His clothes are clearly inadequate for this cold, drear place. But he sings, his eyes on the sky – for he is singing to Apollo, not to them – while his listeners watch, puzzle and dream. Their spears are unnecessary; they are quieted and tamed. The words painted around Orpheus seem to say 'New, new'. As new as the words that Rilke, astonished but obeying, first began to write.

> Da stieg ein Baum. O reine Übersteigung!
> O Orpheus singt! O hoher Baum im Ohr!
> Und alles schwieg. Doch selbst in der Verschweigung
> ging neuer Anfang, Wink und Wandlung vor.

> A tree ascended there. O pure transcendence!
> O Orpheus sings! O tall tree in the ear!
> And all things hushed. Yet in that very silence
> A new beginning, beckoning, change appeared.

Magic chants before his had merely induced oblivion. This was different. When Orpheus sang, he also provoked remembrance. In the listening ear his song opened, grew and began to connect, like a branching tree, lower with higher, men with gods. His music, like all music as Aristotle defined it, transformed the moral character of the soul. As he sang down the decades, barbarians and spear-carriers became peaceful farmers, then city-dwellers, social, civilised and filled with *humanitas*. 'Wild untamed wits,' wrote Sir Philip Sidney, were drawn by him 'to an admiration of knowledge'. Renaissance philosophers especially revered him as the spiritual founder of their walled and towered towns, their piazzas and citizen-summoning bells. He sang confederation, concord and order. In his hymns he sometimes called himself *bukolos*, 'the herdsman', leading stray or savage minds to light.

Shakespeare watched him do this. It began with an act of practised magic: pressing stillness on the world.

> Orpheus with his lute made trees
> And the mountain tops that freeze,
> Bow themselves, when he did sing:
> To his music plants and flowers
> Ever sprung; as sun and showers
> There had made a lasting spring.
>
> Everything that heard him play,
> Even the billows of the sea,
> Hung their heads and then lay by.
> In sweet music is such art,
> Killing care and grief of heart,
> Fall asleep, or hearing, die.

For the ancients, peace was Orpheus's signature. He softened, smoothed and soothed asleep the world of the material and visible. Waves lay down like dogs, barely licking the grey, ridged rocks along the shore. The hills stretched out, and on their breathing sides the long grass bowed and lifted in the sun. His song, in the Greek phrase, 'honeyed the woods'. Men and women who listened forgot the world, entranced into a kind of death. *Fall asleep, or hearing, die.*

But the French writer Paul Valéry, in a poem that deeply impressed Rilke, saw a scene of astonishing upheaval. As Orpheus played, perched on the resplendent rim of the sky, that sky was full of fire and circles of light, and the rocks of the bare mountain rearranged themselves into massive walls of gold. Each charmed stone tottered forward, heaved itself heavenwards, composed a temple. (Rilke too saw this temple, its shifting, shining, precarious stones built up into music in 'inviolable' space.) Out of their enchanted stillness, these objects sprang to life as the poet sang: life visible from life invisible, under the wild sky.

It happened elsewhere. In Orpheus's *Lithica* inert, mute precious stones, empowered by the gods or by a poet's songs, could bring showers or fair weather: polished green jasper pushed up the spring grass, agate filled the wheat ears. A drop of blood-red haematite dust, instilled on a feather, could clear a man's eyes; and one stone made a sound like a baby at its mother's breast, mewing for milk. Only when objects were perceived as *objects*, Coleridge remarked once, were they fixed and dead. The poet saw them as living souls, and thus brought them alive.

One example became famous. As Orpheus strode and

sang one day on the Pimpleian heights, or on Haimon or
Pindus – all mountains in that northern region being part
of his territory – he sensed a rustling and creeping at his
back. Shadows fell unexpectedly, and a chaos of startled birds
beat around him. His holy oaks, the most immovable of trees,
anchored almost to Hades, were following him. One by one
they dragged up their roots, heaving the stony soil, throwing
off the dirt. (The stones followed too, skittering, singing.)
Their broad trunks quivered and grew limber, like the bodies
of stags. Music, his music, coursed through their branches
like new sap, making the toothed leaves shake and shine
under the sun. It flowed, swift as spirit, through the cells to
their green core, along twisted sinews and down polished
defiles of the wrenched-out, dancing wood. From root to
bud his music shivered and surged in them, like release. Their
massed heads moved together, pressing forward, leaving
behind only the dead with their mossy arms stretched out,
wildly tangled in garlands and cloaks of green ivy like half-
dressed mourners abandoned in the street. The living, newly
alive, crashed on.

He led them, then – scarcely daring to turn, in case they
froze behind him – swaying and stumbling from rock to
rock, their canopies full of sky and threshing wings, until
they reached Zonë on the Aegean Sea. There, in an open
space, they arranged themselves in a double ring as though
they meant to dance in a spiral, like the planets around the
sun. But though he urged them to dance, though he challenged them, laughing and splashing, to follow him into the
sea with their hundred hydra arms, they moved no more.
Having staggered so far, astonished by the wide blue glare

ahead of them, they felt the music leave them, and rooted there.

He could lead them only so far. That is still the case.

*

On the Boardwalk in Atlantic City amplified music pumps out with the dawn, whether or not there is anyone to hear it. On this September Sunday, Johnny Cash and Tina Turner boom from Trump's Taj Mahal out over the shining ocean past an audience of stray cats, one woman feeding them, a street-sweeper, a man rolled in a blanket on the sand dunes and two drunks, carrying kites.

They come slowly along the Boardwalk, half-dancing, half-swaying, as the music takes them. Both are middle-aged, with greying beards, pork-pie hats and old stained beachwear they might have picked up in the dunes. But their kites are new. One drunk holds a vinyl dragonfly, red and green with spread wings. The other waves a butterfly, black with bright splotches of yellow, purple and blue. Both also carry cans of beer, balanced with elaborate care. It's a fine day for flying, with a stiff breeze off the Atlantic that whistles in the marram grass and ripples the canopies of the still-sleeping shops. Funnel cake, psychic readings, 'EveryThing 99 Cents', 'Cash for Gold', dreams of sudden fortune under gilt-edged marble domes. The town, the sea and the sky are theirs.

Down the wooden walkway they lurch, towards the Ocean. The going is narrow; they bump each other, curse. One drops his spool of string, setting it bounding over the walkway and through the railings. He turns back for it; the string twines round his legs, half-tripping him. His partner goes on, down to the beach, where the proper force of the wind catches him. He runs a little, delicately, on tiptoe, pointing the nose of his dragonfly into the huge sky, shaking it. His friend sways after him, pumping his right arm up and down, doing the same. But not for one moment do they dare to let their kites go.

Ezra Pound wrote of Li Po, who tried, when drunk, to 'embrace a moon/In the Yellow River'. It's harder to embrace the singing, whirling wind in Atlantic City, if you don't put your beer down first.

*

Socrates declared in Plato's *Phaedrus* that there was nothing to be learned in wild places. But there was a secret language to be read, or sung, in the woods. The Pelasgian alphabet, which Orpheus supposedly used, derived its thirteen consonants from thirteen trees. In order came the birch, the rowan, the ash from the lower slopes of his mountains, his own alder tree and the willow that, touched with a finger, gave him songs sacred to the moon; the hawthorn, the oak, the holly, the hazel shading holy pools, the vine, intoxicating ivy, the elder and the dwarf elder. His leading and luring of trees was perhaps a metaphor for the dance of civilising letters on the page, or for the cycle of leaf-bud and leaf-fall in calendars, to mark out time.

Not only oaks came to him as he sat, singing, on his rock-throne. He drew all trees, from the resistant elm to the sinewy cypress that symbolised rebirth, from the graceful cherry with its mossed, banded bark to the spreading chestnut, the poplar, the vine. The formal plantings of gardens, orange-trees and box and espaliered pear, freed themselves from their pots and painted walls. They formed a theatre round him, meshing branches as though they held hands. In Elizabethan and Stuart England Orpheus was often a gardener, creating from the wilderness circuits of herbs and low hedges, or stately knots of trees.

And not merely trees followed him. The satyrs of Euripides's *Cyclops* thought he knew spells to make dead, burned brands hop out of the fire. His voice 'lured everything by its sweetness', wrote Aeschylus in the *Agamemnon*: everything, pell-mell, nothing left out. Since each creature and object had soul in Orpheus's world, every one was moved. Seneca in his *Hercules Oetaeus* found himself among a crowd of enchanted birds, trees and mountains:

> The woodland brought winged creatures,
> perched in the trees they came;
> but those flying in the open
> veered at the sound of his songs
> with faltering wings, and fell.
> Athos tore its crags free,
> carrying centaurs along,
> and stopped near Rhodope,
> its snows melted by song . . .
> Wild beasts came . . .

Roman mosaic-makers thought the males of each species were drawn to Orpheus especially: the thunderous wild boar creeping now from the bracken, the quick stoat made tentative, the wolf dog-like and cautious. The animal vices of men,

too, were tamed and turned to good. Lion and deer came
together, predator and prey, nuzzling each other's necks. The
crime of devouring living things, said Empedocles, as well as
every bloody act, was outlawed when Orpheus sang. Instead,
'love bound their souls'. Centaurs and satyrs, half-human
passions from the train of Dionysus, left their hoof-marks
around him in the dented grass. The beasts formed a circle of
rapt attention, sometimes a zodiac, waiting to be transformed.

The Emperor Julian thought Orpheus squandered his talent
on wild creatures. He loved them like disciples, and indeed
many were: the birds in particular, singing to Apollo their *tiou,
tiou, tioutinx* in his own mystical willows. All feathered creatures, as well as the bird-like souls who travelled in the air,
turned unresisting to his music. Philostratus said Orpheus drew
not only the sweet singers but the croaking crow, Apollo's bird
of oracle, and the cawing, thieving jackdaw. He lured the star-
tailed peacock of immortality, the unwearying swallows and
the dove of peace, murmuring in laurel leaves. In the quivering silence of the forest, his song over and his lyre laid aside,
he caressed their feathers, from the smallest hopping finch to
the eagle of Zeus, hook-beaked and staring, which carried souls
to heaven. He shared their life, and they shared his. The birds
formed circles round him, on the ground as in the air. He
remarked that they forgot their nests, as men forgot the world.

To many of those who invoked him, singing was all he did.
Like the swain at the end of Milton's *Lycidas*, he sang to the
oaks and streams his 'Doric lay' until the sun set:

> At last he rose, and twitch'd his Mantle blew:
> Tomorrow to fresh Woods and Pastures new.

But that was enough. In Francis Bacon's words:

> Orpheus himself, – a man admirable and truly divine, who
> being master of all harmony subdued and drew all things
> after him by sweet and gentle measures, – may pass by an
> easy metaphor for philosophy personified. For as the works
> of wisdom surpass in dignity and power the works of
> strength, so the labours of Orpheus surpass the labours of
> Hercules.

By his looking and singing alone, the world was changed.
He made the pastures new, the fresh woods; the swirl of his
cloak was in the streaming clouds and the overarching sky.
Such visions were not far from Shakespeare's bringer of spring;
from the poet-creator, as the Romantics saw him; or from
Calderón's conflation in 1634 of singing Orpheus with
creating God, hanging sun and moon in the heavenly vault
and breathing forth the winds:

> *y cruzen el viento, aves*
> *con música y armonía.*

The Romans, in particular, clung to that harmony. As the
empire stumbled to destruction, the whole Orpheus-scene
became a sacred circle of being, as well as a simulacrum of
the *pax Romana* and of concord in the world. Orpheus
acquired a purple mantle and red shoes, the gear of an
emperor whose rule brought transformation out of peace.
And if he were ever to tire and stop playing, as a nervous
Claudian imagined in the fourth century, surely creation
would become Chaos again.

Sculpture by Georgi Chapkanov, Smolyan, 2010

Third string: The sea

He was still a youth, unmarried and impetuous – so Apollonius Rhodius implied when he told the story, around 250 BC – when he was summoned for the voyage of the *Argo* to the land of Colchis, in modern Georgia, to find the Golden Fleece. Chiron, the wisest of the centaurs, had said he should be invited; he had not volunteered. But his name was first on the crew-list, as someone vital to the enterprise. He was already a priest, as well as the ruler of Odrysian Thrace and the Macedonians, a king in his cold country. But it was singing that he was commandeered for. One of the earliest images of him, on a sixth-century BC frieze from Delphi, showed him standing on the *Argo* with his lyre, eager to sail.

Apollonius's account was the most influential and most complete, but it was not the only one. Another was probably composed several centuries earlier, also featuring Orpheus, from which Homer borrowed for the *Odyssey*. Yet another, probably from about 100 BC, claimed to be Orpheus's own narrative of the voyage. In this *Orphic Argonautica* he was recruited for the *Argo* on the brink of old age, pulled reluctantly out of retirement in Thrace; he had already been to the Underworld, and could therefore guide the Argonauts through the horrors of the sea. In the curious, floating chronology of his life, the voyage could happen when anyone pleased. *Comme il vous plaira*. But no other version placed it late – or, for that matter, ever graced him with old age. Universally, he was thought to have died young. The *Argo* voyage therefore fits best, both in terms of his maturing powers and the drama of his life, into some period before his marriage and all that followed.

This voyage meant many things. On the surface it was a challenge to travel among savage tribes, risking death, to bring back treasure. Pelias, King of Iolcus, had devised the task in the hope that Jason, his rival for power, would be distracted or killed on the way; Jason had accepted it, and gathered his crew, for glory, danger, divine favour. But this was also presumed to be the first long voyage made by men out of sight of land. They had knowledge of neither the winds nor the stars, but carried the sons of winds, stars and gods on board, in case they could be useful. They had no maps and no idea of the lands they were aiming at, but instead had built their ship around a log sacred to Athena, goddess of reason, which could think and steer itself. The *Argo* symbolised the human mind reaching out into the unknown.

Scholars have traced their route from Iolcus in Thessaly, through the Hellespont, across the Black Sea to Georgia, then back along the Danube and the Rhône and the west coast of Italy until, with an unwise dip into Libya, they circled via Crete to Greece again. The *Orphic Argonautica*, with a wilder geography, took them as far as the 'boreal Ocean', past Britain and the shores of the Atlantic, into seas bound with ice. But the geography was always notional. This was also a voyage to the unseen places, to dream-realms beyond Earth and life. The journey to Hades — into the self, into death — had its beginnings here.

Orpheus cut a curious figure from the start. Among the fifty-four short-kilted, half-naked heroes who swarmed round the huge ship at Iolcus, where she was drawn up on the beach, he was the only one in long-sleeved, high-belted sacerdotal robes. They were useless for a sea-voyage: embroidered along every seam, weighed down with decorations at the cuffs and hem. He had ridden or walked from Thrace in them, carrying only his lyre. His hair was long, like a god's, and tied back around his brow with ribbons in honour of Dionysus. He wore (by some reports) gold sandals, now dulled with the dust of mountain paths. But he was proud of his holy clothes. All the heroes, Apollonius wrote, gleamed like stars among the clouds: Heracles, Telemon, three sons of Hermes, three sons of Poseidon the sea god and two sons of Zeus, Castor and Pollux, soon to be stars themselves. Orpheus shone especially, the minister of Dionysus and Apollo, the sun striking his bracelets and amulets and shining in the strings of his lyre, as he pressed through the crowd of shouting men and praying, wailing women towards the shore. He himself wrote that the heroes, idling by the ship, sprang up joyfully to greet him as he appeared.

The *Argo* was the first craft built to sail the deep, untravelled sea. Nothing like her had been seen or imagined before. Her hull timbers came from oaks and pines that Orpheus had charmed from the woods; they carried his liberating life in them, and he noted later how she leapt in the sea, like a deer. According to one source he had even built her, but he was seldom allowed that skill. He carried perhaps in a robe-fold or a pocket the useful stone mentioned in his *Lithica*, which would 'return the [shipwrecked] sailor dry-footed to land'. Some said that this stone could make a man walk on water, but he never dealt in miracles of that sort.

At the ship he followed what the others did. Like them he sat on the sand among the huge folded sails, listening closely, as Jason outlined the journey they were to make. A strong twisted rope was girded round the ship, a trench dug before her, rollers laid in the trench, to drag her into the sea. Then Tiphys, the helmsman, leapt on board, wrote Apollonius, 'to urge the youths to push at the right moment':

> and calling on them, he shouted loudly; and they at once, leaning with all their strength, with one push started the ship from her place, and strained with their feet, forcing her onward . . . And then the rollers groaned under the sturdy keel as they were chafed, and round them rose up a dark smoke because of the weight, and she glided into the sea.

By his own account Orpheus sang them on, urging them to shout, strain and pull until their efforts left deep foot-marks in the sand. But they made no progress. The ship 'had its own ideas'. Besides, the keel was clogged by heavy sand and dry seaweed, and Jason asked him to address a song instead to the timbers that made the *Argo*'s hull. So, for the first time on the voyage, Orpheus tuned his lyre and played: not to beasts or men, but to sawn, seasoned planks with the mark of the adze still on them. 'Listen to me again,' he sang. 'Follow me again, through the paths of the virgin sea.' They listened: life coursed through them. Effortlessly, soundlessly, to general astonishment (though not to his), the hull slid down the beach into the waves.

The heroes leapt on board and found their places. Orpheus followed. He had drawn no lots for the massed, gleaming rowing benches, because his task was not to ply oars but to stand before the central mast as the *keleustes*, playing and singing, to keep the rowers going. He made them move and rest, like a life-force; he imposed order, so that the shining oars hit the water and rose as one. If supernatural obstacles appeared, he would draw out their power. He was the ship's talisman against evil. As a Thracian shaman, he would instruct the heroes in the secrets he thought they should know. (For a while, hefty Heracles became his private pupil, bending his giant head to learn poetry.) And whenever they landed, his duty was to organise the rites of Apollo with sacrifice, music and prayer.

The first sacrifice was made as the ship waited, to his precise instructions. They prayed to Apollo as the god of embarkation, soft winds and good sailing. Stones were piled up to make an altar at the edge of the sea, and dried olive wood was spread around it. Barley meal and holy water were sprinkled, and two young steers were flayed, stripped of their fat, cut apart and roasted. Throughout the voyage Apollonius's Orpheus showed no distaste for blood-sacrifice. He was close, even directing, his bare feet slipping in the blood (barefoot, always, for sacrifice), as his comrades slit throats, severed sinews and disengaged the bluish thigh-bones from the flesh. In his own account he killed a bull himself, yanking back the great head to expose the throat; he spread its blood over the altar, ordered the heroes to dip their hands and weapons in the carcass, and mixed a stomach-turning communal drink of blood, barley-flour and sea-water. After the libation he sang the prayer *Ie Paian, ie Paian*, in the required high, slow, steady voice, in his heroic hexameters. The words were supposed to be those of Apollo's mother, Leto, urging her son to shoot his silver bow; they were also Orpheus's theme tune, the daily prayer everyone heard him sing. 'Shoot, boy, shoot, boy,' he sang into the sky. Heal, save and protect us.

The others probably saw him, too, as a mother's boy. He would not cuss or sleep with women, or pull the hard ropes that might burn his hands; the long robes he wore meant effeminacy, as well as holiness. Pherecydes thought it impossible that he was on the voyage; he belonged elsewhere, apart. But Apollonius's Orpheus sat contentedly enough amid the savoury smell of meat roasting, as the black smoke spiralled upwards in good omens and the fires burned all along the shore. If he wanted to ingratiate himself he could perform his party trick of making dead, burned brands hop out of the fire; or he could linger near games of knucklebones, playing innocently, to make the bones shift corner-by-corner towards him or swerve and gyrate in the air, until he was sent politely packing.

Apart from his duties as *keleustes*, however, he may not have fraternised much. Doubtless he spent time practising, enthroned in some corner of the ship where he was out of the way of men and ropes. And he continued with his curious interests, noticing not only the strange tribes, but, especially, the new plants and trees they found. The sacred grove where the Fleece hung was, to him, mostly of interest for the medicinal flowers that grew there: asphodel, plantain, maidenhair fern, thorn-apple, galingale, delicate vervain, sage, mustard, cyclamen, lavender, cup-shaped peony (Apollo's salve), camomile, saffron and white hellebore. All these were useful as antidotes or for spells. Where the heroes went ashore to gallivant, or sometimes to kill, he went to pick things, emerging with strange posies in his hands.

Certain members of the crew seem to have caught his eye. Hylas, the boyfriend of Heracles, impressed him for the white smoothness of his cheeks, glowing with just a little pink and shaded with ginger down. He noticed also the two 'beautiful' sons of the north wind that ruled in Thrace. The most descriptive of his hymns was addressed to that wind, Boreas:

> bringer of freezing winter winds, shaker of the air!
> Leave snowy Thrace behind you once again –
> dissolve the rebellious damp and darkening clouds,
> whip up the water to rushing drops of rain . . .

Any Thracian knew that cold, wet scene. As for the boys, Calais and Zetes, they had arrived on board in a downdraught of fierce air, dusky wings wrapping them from neck to ankle and glinting with gold scales. Their long, dark hair had tossed and tangled as they fell. Later they rushed together in pursuit of the scavenging Harpies, thrashing at their wings with swords and grabbing them with their hands, high above the Floating Islands. They came back breathless, boasting, bedraggled. Little obviously connected Orpheus, prince, priest and lyre-player, with the wild wind-children. But the northern boys clung together.

At dusk on the day of embarkation, as the rocky hills threw their shadows across the ploughed fields, the heroes ate their first meal as a company. Orpheus lay, like them, on heaped-up silvery olive leaves at the edge of the sea, almost in the surf, drinking unmixed sweet wine until his head spun. Inevitably, some of the men began to quarrel. Others restrained them by force, but Orpheus instead jumped up, unsteady himself, and began singing. It was instinctive. Human savagery could be tamed by sacred song as the animals had been.

What he sang was his most famous piece, the *Song of Creation*. His mother, he said, had taught it to him; it was perfumed with her divinity and her enfolding tenderness. His whole reputation rested on this poem, said Diodorus: 'a wonderful thing, which excelled in its melody when it was sung'. He was to perform it several times on the voyage, whenever his power was most needed, as medicine or prayer.

Sitting on a rock among the heroes, he laid both hands to the strings. He began softly, mistily, with 'Chaos and beloved Night' coexisting in darkness. Gradually, strongly, light was flung out of his lyre as the gods emerged and struggled. Earth was ripped from Heaven, sea from Earth. Sky stretched out, like a canopy, to the limits of the universe. He played louder, fixing the paths of sun, moon and stars and raising the mountains, note above note, rock over rock, especially his Thracian peaks. He made rivers, rushing from string to string with pealing sweeps of the plectrum, and nymphs of woods and water delicately treading, as lightly as he could sing. Fiercely then, shocking them with his change of mood, he sang of wars in Heaven against Kronos, 'the terrible destroyer', and the downfall of the giants into the waves of Ocean; he sang of Rhea completing creation and endlessly bestowing life, the bringer of winds and fair weather. From that point he simply improvised, like a freshening breeze among the strings.

Every part of his hymn was praise. Every line offered creation back to the Creator. That, as he sang through Rilke, was what a poet was for:

> *Rühmen, das ists! Ein zum Rühmen Bestellter,*
> *ging er hervor wie das Erz aus des Steins*
> *Schweigen. Sein Herz, vergängliche Kelter*
> *eines des Menschen unendlichen Weins.*

> Praise, that's the thing! As a praiser and blesser
> he came, ringing ore from the stone-silent mine.
> Came to press out from his heart, only mortal,
> A never-to-die, inexhaustible wine.

As he sang the heroes leaned forward to hear him, silent as stone themselves. And long after he had ceased, quickly pulling the strings away from the plectrum, they went on listening to the lingering air; to the unaccustomed echo of beauty in their hearts. Orpheus had sung for them the forgotten song of their souls.

> *Und alles schwieg. Doch selbst in der Verschweigung*
> *ging neuer Anfang, Wink und Wandlung vor.*

> And all things hushed. Yet in that very silence
> A new beginning, beckoning, change appeared.

The next dawn they left the harbour by oars alone, the sail unraised. As the hawsers were slipped, wine was poured on the sea as a libation. Orpheus had taken up his station in the moving prow of the ship. With one sandalled foot he beat the planks of the deck, steadily, not too fast. 'To the sound of his lyre,' wrote Apollonius, 'they smote with their oars the rushing sea-water, and the surge broke over the blades; and on this side and on that the dark brine seethed with foam, boiling terribly with the might of the heroes, and their arms shone in the sun like flame.' The sight filled Orpheus's eyes, a glittering army of rowers in the cauldron of the sea. Then the west wind caught them, 'benevolent, swift-whirling power', as he invoked it in his own Mysteries: bearer of souls, bringer of breath, filler of the new, adventuring sails. 'Tiphys dared,' wrote Seneca in his *Medea*:

> to spread his canvas on the vast waste sea
> and write new laws for the winds:
> now to strain the ropes with sails full-bellied,
> now to advance
> one sheet to catch the cross-winds,
> now to set
> the yards safely at mid-mast . . .
> while above the lofty sail
> the scarlet topsails tremble.

At this point Orpheus could stop his rowing music, watching instead from the prow as the misty cornfields of the Pelasgians faded, and the boundless blue horizon opened out before him.

He had sailed before, to Egypt, but that had been a case of hugging the coast and keeping the shore in view. The landscape of the deep sea was new to him, as it was to all of them. He was the first mortal to sing of it, and in 'his own' account he did so in special, awe-filled words. This was a 'vastness', almost one with the vast sky, which nonetheless boiled and foamed, white on blue, like a whirlpool – for creation still whirled in circles, even here. The wide main was 'the end of the earth, the beginning of all', an *abyssos*, much like Chaos before creation came. His sea was very seldom 'unharvested', as Homer's was: in the *Hymns* and the *Lithica* the depths of it, 'glossy' and 'black', like Night herself, writhed with potential and with new forms swimming into life. He sang with special fascination of the *kouralion*, or coral, born as a plant in the sea-deeps, so delicate, so light, paddling to the surface like a small creature and then, tired of swimming, turning into stone as it rested under the clear 'sky-air' on the shore. The waves, too, were 'Poseidon's flowers', budding, blooming and dissolving in a turmoil of white. Repeatedly he fell back on the word *apletos*: extraordinary, immense, ungraspable, unfathomable. But as he stood at the rail, fingering his ship-wreck-stone and grappling with the queasiness of the land-lubber, a hymn and its melody began to grow at the sea's edges: bringing it into his body like breath, making it his.

> To thee, Poseidon, fell by lot
> the unfathomable sea;
> the waves and their wild denizens,
> the ships that speed on thee;
> O spirit of the rippling deep,
> our great protector be.

As the vessel ran quietly past the northern coast, the long, strong rhythms of his song urged the boat on before the wind. The *Argo* was entranced and silent, caught in his music as though he held the form of 'impetuous Athena', helmeted and wilful as he imagined her, subdued for a moment in his arms.

Fish followed him, from minnows to whales, snaking in silent vortices in the turquoise sea. He shared their life, and they shared his. Birds hovered above him, halcyon and gull wheeling slowly on a thermal of sound, and into their light element – as into new waves – the fish leapt too, flashing and listening. Seals swam with him, their large eyes full of tears.

His song was of Artemis, the Thracian moon goddess and guardian of the mountains by the coast. Between Orpheus and the moon there was an understanding. He called his disciples 'sons of the light-bearing moon', rather than sun-children. Her cloak of yellowish clouds he saw as the gossamer saffron-veiling of a bride, 'pinned with a brooch of amber' as he, in the Thracian way, wore his. She might come as his own bride. The name *Argo*, 'white-shimmering', was a synonym for the moon; and perhaps, with his music, he could draw her too down to the water.

Yet his adoration had a darker side. In 'his own' version of the voyage he also worshipped the moon as Hecate, the three-faced goddess of the Underworld, night and the dead. He was said to have introduced her Mysteries among the tribes of the Aegean as he passed. She was invoked in the first of his hymns, lovely yet repellent, haunting deserted places in a long, swishing cloak, revelling in tombs. Her white pockmarked disc rose at each crossroads, presiding mutely over all decisions; she was in charge of the course the ship took and of the pull of the tides. Chillingly, she shone in the churned-up wake by the stern; serenely, she lit a glimmering path amid the vast, teeming night-plains of the sea.

He knew the moon contained mountains, cities and mansions; his longing gaze could discern them. But, whether Artemis or

Hecate, it was her changing light that engrossed him. She was made, he wrote, of the whitest particles of all, atoms as cold as she was. Among the 'crowd of books' attributed to him was one called *The Phases of the Moon*. He mentioned especially, said Clement of Alexandria, the new moon, the fifteen-day moon and the thirtieth: the 'three-way shining' of her white robes first increasing, then diminishing. His calendars of crop-planting were based on her. The seven phases she passed through corresponded to the seven strings of his lyre. And her seventh phase was invisible, the end of six phases of manifestation, swallowed up by the dark out of which her dim horns grew again.

The *Argo* paused first on the island of Lemnos, opposite the coast of Thrace. Orpheus called it 'holy', but it did not seem so. The night was spent in a city of moon-shining towers in which the women had killed all the men. They wore bronze armour for fear of Thracian invaders, but the heroes calmly unbuckled it and slept with them. (Athena too wore armour, and perhaps that too could be removed, piece by piece, to find her white, pure body, like a whittled branch.) Artemis presided over a city of whispers, of quickly slammed shutters, dowsed lights and sighing streets. Through these Thracian Orpheus wandered alone, but for her cool gaze on him.

He knew in principle the allure and fecundity of women, for all his goddesses possessed it, and their loves were part of the ebb and flow of everything there was. He was not an innocent, exactly. But he was nervous when the heroes failed to return. When they did not come for days, he sang a 'bewitching song' with 'preserving words', simply to compel them, whether they wanted to or not. Then he took them away to Samothrace to be purified.

They landed there, at the mouth of his own Hebrus, as evening fell. He alone knew the secrets of the Cabiri, the unruly ancient earth-spirits or 'great gods' of that place. Sailors did well to invoke them. He therefore initiated the heroes into 'terrifying' Mysteries – he said no more – 'that they might sail more safely over the chilling sea'. The bowls they dedicated in the sacred precinct remained there, Diodorus said, for many years. Round each muscled waist Orpheus tied, tightly, the red belt of an initiate. A finger on their lips pledged the heroes to secrecy in that incense-thick night, on the level sand. At his instruction they 'closed the gates', as when gold foil was laid in thin hammered sheets across the lips and eyes of the Thracian dead.

He could enforce purity; and he could stir up life, too, if that was necessary. When the heroes murdered the king of the Doliones, a Black Sea tribe, he made them propitiate the great Nature goddess, leading them up Mount Dindymum, Rhea's mountain, to leave a primitive wood carving of her propped beside an altar of small stones. It was a Thracian offering, the sort he would have made as a boy in the forest: finding the face of the goddess in a branch or a stone and polishing it, carefully, with his blue cloak, before dedicating it at some holy spot among the trees. But she responded to him differently, more prodigally, than she had then. Fruit suddenly appeared on the trees and bushes, swelled, softened and fell; red apples unbruising in the grass, blackberries that stained their hands. Where water had never flowed before, a cold stream shone, trickled, gushed from the rocks. They had been forgiven.

After this he also told the younger heroes to dance in full

armour, drumming, shouting, to smother the Doliones' lamentations for their king. He made them dance like Thracians, or like Dionysian revellers. Weeping had to be drowned out with crashing sword on shield, as the Kouretes had danced around crying baby Zeus in his Cretan cave, and as they circled him still in the depths of intelligible Heaven. Brass-sounding, drum-beating life had to be summoned up instead.

Then he made the crew be quiet again. After energy and noise, he imposed calm and peace. Whenever necessary, he played music of healing: after scraps and battles, when wounds were dressed. He knew remedies, if they needed them, such as pounded haematite and honey smeared as a salve on cuts; he had learned that one in Egypt. But his songs themselves could be a *pharmakon*, a magic drug that slowed, like Apollo's scarlet peony juice, the flow of blood in the body. On the coast of Bebrycia once he played a chant to which the heroes sang in harmony, lying in the dusk beneath bay trees to which the hawsers had been tied, while bay-leaf crowns perfumed their hands and hair. The chant wound on and on, as his chants tended to, ending in drowsy prayers.

On many occasions his music softened his companions to tenderness or reflection. (Monteverdi, too, writing his *Orfeo* in 1607, said Orpheus had moved him to 'proper prayer'.) But his songs could also revive and energise, pushing the heroes to feats even they thought impossible. Sometimes both those powers seemed to be in play: a death-like enchantment, the wild surge of life. In the Bosphorus, according to Apollonius, only his shrill-sung commands forced the *Argo* through the twin clashing stacks of the Symplegades that towered over them and threatened in moments to destroy them, foam and water crashing 'up to the stars', the heroes pulling when he told them, barely resting, pulling again with roars of exertion, while their huge oars bent like bows. But Orpheus himself said his part in this was to charm the rocks, persuading them not to smash in fury but to drift gently apart, using a song his mother knew.

After a while, when he feared it less, he could also calm the sea. Roped fast in the pitching, heaving bow, he would fling out his hymns to the mounting walls of the waves. They would pause, though not immediately: not yet with a river's obedience, but sulkily and turbulently, their huge grey backs humped up beside him, still flecking out spume in the north-west 'Thracian' winds. Note by note he would urge them lower, resist them, coax them, until his music streamed down them in foam and they deflated, slowly, to a cradling quiet. His spirit lay on the sea then, pressing it level like a band of light.

Those frightening Cabiri of Samothrace, Diodorus thought, had given him powers to make the wind drop and the stars to fall over the water as a sign the heroes would be safe. On one occasion in the Black Sea, when his songs, again, had tethered the winds and smoothed the waves, the sea god Glaucus swam alongside, streaming with weed and barnacled like the hull of a boat, to call him by name and commend him.

Philostratus described another painting of Orpheus 'beguiling the sea'. He sang to it softly, while circling kingfishers sang to him.

Inevitably his thoughts kept returning to Apollo. The Golden Fleece itself, towards which they sailed, was a token of him.

Apollo spoke to him directly, all the time, pricking and goading him with inspiration, pushing him to sing the truth. The sun god's sacrificial tripod – the bronze three-footed cauldron in which he had gathered the shining scraps of Dionysus, later displayed at Delphi – was in Orpheus's keeping. When wine was mixed in it and sipped from it he could take on the god, his lips suddenly twitching and shouting with prophecies, but he did not reveal that mystery on this voyage. He slept perhaps with one arm curled around it, protecting it, while the other cloaked and cradled the warm shell of his lyre. The tripod was offered to the gods at Lake Tritonis in North Africa, almost at the end of the voyage, to ensure a safe return, find a way out; young Triton seized it in his cold, webbed hands. The last Orpheus saw of it was a bronze gleam in the great salt lake, before it was taken to the depths. Much as he longed to protect it, he had to let it go. But at Callichorus on the Pontic coast, where Dionysus had paused to establish rites on his way back from India, Orpheus dedicated his lyre, or perhaps rededicated it, to the god of the sun: the far-shooter, the all-seeing, 'borne aloft on golden wings'.

A little before, on the bare island of Thynias in the Black Sea, he had watched with the others as Apollo rose with the dawn. The heroes had rowed all night, so he had sung to inspire them, sinking to hoarse half-sleep as the day appeared. Exhausted, the crew beached the ship 'at the time when divine light has not yet come nor is it utter darkness, but a faint glimmer has spread over the night'. There Apollo appeared to them, his quiver and arrows gleaming, throwing off the light from his golden hair across the sea and along the shore. The perfume of powdered frankincense blew with him as he rose, and the waves roared. If this was his father who strode among the fire-fringed clouds, Orpheus was no more able than any of the heroes to look him in the face. Instead, astonished, like them, he bent his head to the earth in silence.

After a while, he spoke. 'Come,' he said, the word a cough of emotion in his throat. 'Let us call this island the sacred isle of Apollo of the Dawn, since it was then that he appeared to us.'

They agreed.

'Let's offer whatever sacrifices we can, building an altar here on the shore. And if we're granted a safe return, then we will offer the thighs of goats to him. Let's offer libations to him now.' He raised his arms to the ever-brightening sky. 'Be gracious, O king, be gracious / when you appear to us.'

At his command the heroes raised an altar of stones, went hunting for wild goats in the woods, wrapped the thigh-bones in fat and offered them. Again, blood-sacrifice did not trouble him. Around the sacrifice they set up a dancing ring, circling and singing to Apollo as the god of healing. Orpheus made a new song for them of the god as a boy among the rocks of Mount Parnassus, slaying the monster Delphyne, half-maiden, half-snake, with his golden arrows. He sang too, because the vision was still fresh, of Apollo's golden hair shaken out like light, how he tossed it and delighted in it, and how it was never to be cut, only caressed by his mother 'with her dear hands' – as Calliope, perhaps, had once caressed his. The sun rose steadily, pleased with the singer and the song.

Nor was this the last encounter. Sailing in the Cretan Sea

on the way home, 'Night scared them, that night which they call the fall of Darkness'. The heroes could not tell whether dark had slid from Heaven, or risen from the depths; whether it was Chaos, or Hades, through which they were carried blindly by the sea. Orpheus's music could not help them this time. Though he revered the dark, he also feared it; he did not know what to do, how to respond. They seemed about to wreck on the Melantian rocks, solid bulk rearing suddenly out of pitch-black water and air, but Jason called on Apollo to save them. He came at once, with his god's alacrity, lighting up with the dazzle of his bow a tiny island in the Sporades. When they landed dawn rose at once, as if he had lit the sky only for their sake.

They called the island Anaphe, 'Apparition', and worshipped Apollo among the trees. Orpheus, again, presided. His own power was so small and weak by comparison, so uncontrolled, like the faltering steps of a child. He sang the *Ie Paian, ie Paian*, high and slowly, as required. But, as at Thynias, this dawn was not a moment for canticles. It was a time – Rilke could have told him of it, pressing his hand with fervour – for words deeper than language, 'speech-seeds' wrapped in heart's innermost silence, in which 'the perfect Hymn to the Sun would have to be composed'.

*

Rabindranath Tagore, Bengal's greatest poet, also saw that sky. At the dawn of the twentieth century he stood on the shore of the wide, flat Jalumna where it flowed into the sea, past riverine pastures where cattle grazed and tall palms stood in rows. For days in his house he had strung and unstrung the instrument of his heart, waiting for the Master's touch and his footstep, knowing that 'I am here to sing thee songs' and that only as a singer could he come before the Presence; but feeling that the tune, the time, the words, were not yet right.

Now, out on the morning water, boats strained at their moorings on bamboo poles; women walked out slowly into the dawn with brass pots on their heads. And above blazed immortal Love, 'shimmering from sky to sky', a golden harp whose music made the gold and silver, blue and green of the water and the air. In miniature, leaping but barely tuned, his own heart followed. 'With the tune of thee and me,' he wrote, 'all the air is vibrant.'

Inevitably, though, there was sorrow in it. 'It is the pang of separation', he wrote:

> that spreads throughout the world and gives birth to shapes innumerable in the infinite sky . . . It is this overspreading pain that deepens into loves and desires . . . and this it is that ever melts and flows in songs through my poet's heart.

He could not cross the river or attempt the shoreless ocean, his songs the pulsing waves, alone. But on a later occasion, in a dusk of July, with the monsoon clouds massed above him and the lightning already flickering, something drew him from the house. The glades in the *bakula* grove where he had played as a child, hearing songs beyond the cooing doves that had led him to the depth of mysteries, lay quiet. Shutters were closed, streets silent. No one passed by; only the wind was up, and ripples 'rampant in the river'.

But there at the ford sat a man in a small boat, holding a harp in his hands.

*

Apollonius's Orpheus never viewed the Golden Fleece on its oak tree in Colchis, guarded by a sleepless dragon. When they reached the sacred grove, he did not enter. He saw the Fleece only when Jason brought it back in triumph, the wire-tufts so bright that they flamed in his cheeks and cast a flickering sheen on the ground. The Fleece had appeared on the tree, Apollonius wrote, dazzling like the lightning of Zeus: as Orpheus would have said, like the soul in man. To retrieve that light seemed a task he might have tried. But this was Jason's own initiation: to yoke the flame-breathing, bronze-hoofed oxen, to plough the field of Ares, the war god, and sow it with serpents' teeth, to kill the armed men that sprang up shouting from them, to enter the grove of terror where Fleece and dragon hung. Orpheus had none of that strength, had never felt his sharp sword enter a man, could not even muster the necessary anger. In silence, like the others, he waited on board the *Argo* for Jason to return. Only at night – his longed-for, particular time – could he sit alone beside the cloak-wrapped Fleece, fingers tentatively brushing the deep, oil-soft brightness, prayers forming on his lips.

Yet in his own version of the voyage he fetched the Fleece himself, through different terrors. The heroes begged him to placate Artemis-Hecate, the moon goddess of death, who guarded the grove with her white pockmarked face. Reluctantly he agreed to go with Jason and three others. They were followed at some distance by a strange, intense girl, who clutched to her breast a fistful of poisonous plants. This was Medea. She was the daughter of Hecate and King Aietes, to whom the Fleece belonged; she had fallen in love with Jason, and had fled away with him. In most versions of the story, it was she who charmed the dragon into relinquishing the Fleece. In Orpheus's version she was useful, but it was he who made the difference.

All was done in a rush; time was short. At the edge of the sacred grove, hard by the locked silver gates, Orpheus dug a triple ditch to propitiate Hecate's three forms. In it he lit a fire of oily, spirit-conjuring juniper, perfumed cedar, buckthorn and weeping poplar, the tree of death. He made figurines of barley-flour and water, scrabbling with sticky, mealy hands, and dropped them in the fire. Then he killed three black puppies – sacred to Hecate – mixed their blood with vitriol, soapwort, plantain, alkanet and saffron, all growing nearby, and threw the limp fur bundles on the pyre. Night ruled now, dim with stars. Pulling on black robes, veiling his head so that he saw almost nothing, he picked up a bronze shield to summon the goddess to him.

As soon as he struck, the Earth split open. Out came the three Furies, their dry pine torches spilling red light. The ditch roared up with exploding smoke, sparks and flame in which loomed, suddenly, Pandora, with a body made of iron. With her came 'a being of changing shape . . . monstrous, inconceivable', with the heads of a long-maned mare, a she-dog and a snake. In her hands she held swords. He recognised this as Hecate, fresh from Hell. As she circled his ditches, the statue of Artemis that guarded the gates let the torches fall from her hands. The gates slid back, and Orpheus ran into the vast, dark, holy wood.

He glimpsed the oak, as tall as the sky, with the Fleece like a beacon there. The dragon was coiled, wakeful, in huge rings around the tree. It unwound itself and raised its head 'with a deathly roar that made the ineffable Aether ring, and the trees shake to their roots'. Here Orpheus paused. He had fought such a dragon before, with a sappy, half-burned branch, at the mouth of a cave, his child's legs shaking; if Apollo had not intervened, he would have died. He was terrified. But there was careful work to do, music-work, as the whole wood groaned around him:

> I tuned up the divine voice of my lyre and, playing on the deepest string, intoned a muffled chant without sounding the words. My lips moved silently. I was invoking Sleep, the universal sovereign of gods and men, asking him to exercise his charm on the dragon. At once he responded, flying on golden wings, putting to sleep as he came the transient tribes of men, the impetuous winds, the waves of the sea, the unwearying springs and the courses of rivers, the beasts and the birds, all that lives and all that dies.

As he sang, the dragon slowly collapsed its great neck along the ground. It fell asleep, weighed down beneath its own gleaming scales. Jason and the others rushed forward to hook the Fleece down from the oak-boughs, rustling and shining like a soft sluice of coins.

But this was not the end of their trials. As they sailed near Campania and Sicily on the way home, a sound of alternative singing came from the waters. They were passing the Isle of the Sirens. Odysseus, voyaging this way later, was lashed to the mast and had his ears stuffed with wax to resist the voices that rose from the island, shimmering like the play of a hundred harps all softly struck at once. The Sirens meant to lure the Argonauts there to die, leaving their bones to moulder on the sand. Their music, like Orpheus's, contained divine ratios and the harmony of the spheres; it seemed as beautiful to untrained ears; but it led only to oblivion, the earthly sleep of the soul. Their songs stroked tirelessly across a man's skin, wave after unguent wave, suggesting what he might see, touch, feel, love: the fascination of death by sensuality and by distraction.

For a while the song was still distant, the singers unseen. These were women, perhaps; possibly, as Orpheus himself suggested, only two of them, reclining on the high cliffs of their island, one with a reed pipe and the other with a lyre. Some saw them as painted birds with fantails and spotted breasts beneath their women's faces. But his mother Calliope and the other Muses had outsung them, stripping them of their feathers and leaving only their melody to clothe them.

The *Argo* resisted this no better than any other craft. She let herself be carried so near the island, rocking gently on that delicious sea, that the ropes were made ready to land. But Orpheus had been recruited especially for this. He would be pure, unimpressed, unaffected; and he needed no bidding to compete. He rushed to the deck-rail, already frantically turning the pegs in the cross-bar, for only the most perfect tones could rival these. But something wrapped around him there, a silken shawl of sound, tactile and unexpected. With it came the perfume of lilies, Apollonius said, and the feel of their petals, soft, cool, white. It swathed him from the tender base of the ear to the collarbone, to the breast, ever more loving and imploring. His blood slowed and tingled in his endlessly branching veins, no part escaping. He was bound to listen; he could not block it out, and his mortal flesh could not necessarily resist it.

He lifted his lyre; already he was hardly aware of it, as if he was dreaming. Already his body seemed to be dissolving, to be entered by softly beating sound-waves, to be losing breath. He found himself erect, hardening. It was vital to ignore this, to find the notes. Unconscionably, his fingers stumbled. Lily-soft hands of song caressed him in a way he had never felt, never imagined. He might faint away here, his body falling along the rail and sliding into the sea. He would not care.

The Siren-music swam at the ship's side, quivering sheets flung up again and again to draw her close like a hawser. One hero, Butes, his mind melting, sprang from his polished bench and leapt into the sea. It was all Orpheus could do not to follow his floundering wake, not to hear. But he tried to struggle, and his first notes fought for him, small glittering rips and slashes in his silken shroud, until he was breathing, gasping, almost free. His music became a honed blade, a hail of bright stones flung at the swaddled water, scimitars of light.

Finding his voice at last, he began to sing. Again, he said later, it was his mother who prompted him. He sang of Zeus and Poseidon arguing over thunder-hooved horses, and of how furious Poseidon, tossing his blue mane of hair, had pounded the land of Lycaon into the islands where they now sailed. It was the song of a sea-storm; he could play such music expertly now. The waves and the west wind came to his aid then, said Apollonius, pushing the ship on. The Siren voices began to fret and fade, beaten into retreat.

He drew back from the rail, where tags of their song still

floated. Victory was his, of a sort. The sea threatened nothing else, though its wide, trembling blue seemed to come too close, like a girl's stare. He was still disturbed by this sort of love, and by this sort of Death.

He saved the Argonauts once more, in Libya in the African desert. (That desert, where Jung's soul led him in 1915, was perhaps for Orpheus too the wide landscape of himself, 'where only the sun of unquiet desire burned'.) They had been swept off-course for home, finding themselves suddenly in a sea of shoals, thick seaweed and foam that broke without sound. They were at the edge of a vast land 'stretching far, like a mist', empty of water or paths. Wrapped in their cloaks, squalid with dust and thirst, the crew wandered desperately over the sands, heaving the *Argo* with them. Orpheus might have remembered then that his putative father was also the most deadly of the gods; his arrows killed.

Where grassland began to invade the sand, in tufts and dull green mats, a strange scene appeared: an overgrown garden, and in it a tree of apples that changed with the colours of the sunset, from yellow, to pink, to bluish-crimson, to pure gold. Orpheus knew – even before touching them, or daring to twist one quickly from the stalk for that sweet, saving mouthful of juice – that these were the apples of death and rebirth that had been placed in the cradle of Dionysus. They were surely not to be eaten, only offered, and their fragrance inhaled on the altar. He had reached the land of the 'sweet-voiced Hesperides', at the western edge of the world.

Beside the tree its guardian serpent lay dead, with black flies clustering in its wounds. The stench was awful. Around

it the three Hesperides, the nymphs who were charged with
the keeping of the apple-garden, raised their white arms in
lamentation above their golden heads. As the heroes
approached, however, they subsided at once to earth and dust.
They became Death.

For a while, astonished, no one spoke. Then Orpheus, stepping forward, spoke for them. He alone understood the
nymphs' transformation, and knew that the sandy ground
before him was suddenly holy and alive. This time, he did not
sing or play. Instead he prayed to these 'divine ones' – whether
from Heaven or the Underworld, he did not know – to manifest themselves, and show them water.

His voice, without the lyre, sounded faint and despairing.
But it was heard. Grass sprouted in the dust, then tall shoots,
then saplings from which the star-maidens gazed on them,
'perfectly contained': a willow, a poplar, a wide-hipped elm.
They were caught in the forms of girls bending, turning,
flexing their delicate hands. Their leaves giggled at him. But
their branching arms also pointed to a far place where water,
veined with light, gushed from the rocks. Orpheus raced
there with the others, sobbing as mud sucked at his aching
feet, soaking his face with the delicious, prodigal coolness,
cramming his mouth until water cascaded over his body.
Behind them the trees became maidens again, and the maidens
stars.

He would have realised here – looking up at last, water
dripping from his chin – the limits of his power. He could
calm the winds, but could not unleash them; he could stop
streams, make them follow him, stroke them flat like cloth,
but could not make them appear. He was a poet and a

magician, a semi-god, halfway divine. Very seldom did anyone suggest he was more than that.

He took three golden apples away from the Hesperides. They reminded him of his trials, his thirst and the skin-tingling song of the maidens who had become trees. They glowed in their wooden box and perfumed it, holy things.

Three other events from the voyage were worth recording. As the heroes fled with the Golden Fleece, King Aietes pursued them with his fleet. He was anxious to recover both the Fleece and his daughter, Medea, from Jason's arms. In Medea Orpheus had a rival of sorts, who knew from her moon-witch mother how to kill or stupefy with poisonous plants, and how to stay the courses of rivers and the stars. He grudgingly admired her knowledge, though she had come on board half-hysterical and with scratch-marks on her face; she was clearly powerful, but also bad luck, and silence was the only way to deal with girls like that. Later she was to roam his own Mount Pangaion, snipping venomous herbs with a sharp, darting fingernail. And in the end she had saved him, spiriting him and the others out of Colchis alive. 'My gift was Orpheus,' said Seneca's Medea later, justifying in a single point her treacherous career. She had preserved him and his life-giving music for the world. He never thanked her.

He sang, however, at her hastily improvised wedding to Jason in the land of the Phaeacians. Outside the nuptial cave he stood and played like an usher, green leaves twisted round his hair, while inside it the Golden Fleece, covered with flowers and fine linen, was spread to make a bridal bed.

Night took charge again; discreetly he muffled his lyre, and left them. When dawn came, and the local women brought gold ornaments and jars of wine to the bride, he strolled up to play once more, 'beating the ground with his gleaming sandal', as the circling nymphs sang round him. Every time he reached the word 'marriage' they began the bridal chant again, an endless invocation. But life renewed itself always; the dance could not stop. The next marriage he attended, as it happened, would be his own. The golden apples in his box were omens, too, of that.

Seneca added another scene. King Aietes had laid a curse on the whole crew; Orpheus had removed it with purifying rites. To distract the pursuers, Medea had then murdered her half-brother, dismembered him and fed his bloody pieces to the ravening waves. Perhaps Orpheus refused to look at this *sparagmos* reddening the sea, over which birds and ships fought together. If he gave way, despite himself, to curiosity, it was his own death he saw.

At the end of the voyage, as the heroes disbanded, Orpheus by 'his own' account slipped away to the gorge of Taenarus, at the southernmost tip of the Peloponnese. The chasm here, he knew, ran right through the Earth, 'bottomless and without foundation'. Steep, foggy forests disappeared into the depths, a terror with, this time, no gleam of the Fleece within it. The gate at Taenarus was as close as he could get to Hades. There, risking it, quite alone, he sacrificed to the gods of the lower world. Only a few steps more, and he would have entered. But this time he was not ready, or had no excuse. That was to come.

Roman copy of Attic bas-relief, fifth-century BC

Middle string: Love

Her name was Eurydice. She came slowly, appearing around the end of the fifth century BC and acquiring her name much later. She came quietly: her only recorded words were sighs of pain. She was never really a woman, always an allegory, sketchy and unsatisfactory. The Greeks barely needed her; her fame grew in more sentimental times. But without her Orpheus was myth rather than man, a shaman who went to the Underworld merely because he could. Eurydice made him human. At the same time she brought him to realise, slowly, what Love was, what Death was, and what his destiny was meant to be.

Orpheus's love for her also marked a change, Rilke thought, in his vocation as a poet. To gaze on creation and remake it in song was only the beginning of his work. He had to go deeper:

> For looking, you see, has a limit.
> And the more looked-at world
> wants to be nourished by love . . .

Now practise heart-work
on those images captive within you; for you
overpowered them only, but now do not know them.
Look, inward man, look at your inward maiden,
her the laboriously won
from a thousand natures, at her the
being till now only
won, yet never loved.

The Greeks thought of Eurydice as a dryad, a tree-spirit. Orpheus could not escape trees. She was perhaps the sensuous flickering of the willow or the drifting cotton-whiteness of the poplar; the slim, shocking nakedness of the silver birch against a rock; the fir with its upturned, draping branches, gracefully demanding attention, or the pinkish pallor left beneath the bark of a plane tree, like a girl's misted face in a mirror. He had seen her shadow already in the Hesperides. She was assumed to be Thracian, from the woods he knew. As he saw her within the tree, and sang to her gently in his high, light voice, earth lost its grip on her; her branches softened, her trunk warming and smoothing under his hands as the bark receded. He hung her with necklaces and breathed freedom into her, kiss by touch by kiss.

Calderón in the seventeenth century returned to this theme. His Eurydice was human nature, *Naturaleza Humana*, made by Orpheus in his image to be united with him in love. Inside a rock she lay curled asleep until his singing roused her – as it had already wakened light, winds and stars, the beasts and the birds. 'What power is this,' she asked, sleepily stirring, 'whose singing transforms me from not being into being?' Unresisting, she turned like a flower towards the invisible lover who had called her into life.

Rilke, too, saw her that way, curled within himself as in a tree. She was 'an almost-girl', *ein Mädchen fast*: his Vera, hovering between life and death. Like in-held breath, she waited; swathed in spring gauzes, like a girl in a Botticelli painting, she dreamed Nature and existence there, 'sleeping the world':

> *Und alles war ihr Schlaf.*
> *Die Bäume, die ich je bewundert, diese*
> *fühlbare Ferne, die gefühlte Wiese*
> *und jedes Staunen, das mich selbst betraf.*

> And all things were her sleep:
> all trees I ever gazed on, every shape,
> the spaces, meadows, tangible and real,
> and every wonder I myself could feel.

Eurydice had slept thus, the poet's own *anima* or feminine soul, entranced by the visible and sensual, never wishing to be woken.

> How, God of Song, did you
> Create her never to desire awakening?
> Was she set here only to sleep, to dream?

> Where is her death now? Ah, will you discover
> this theme in time, before your songs decay?
> Almost a girl, where does she drift away? . . .

Her names, though, suggested a profounder history. At first she was Agriope, 'the voice of the wild fields' or 'the gleaming face'; by the first century BC she was Eurydice, 'wide-ruling'. These were names also given to Persephone, the Queen of night and death. Death indeed was her theme, then, as much as life. Persephone too first appeared as a careless girl in a meadow, filling her arms with pale narcissi, yellow, gold and white, garlanding her fair hair with the faint, sweet, wet scent of them, before Pluto snatched her down to the realms below the earth. There she became the adjudicator of death, life and rebirth, and the keeper of their mysteries.

Before Eurydice was named as his love, Persephone was the only woman Orpheus seemed to care for. Three poems about her abduction were attributed to him; they were read and performed every night in the rites he presided over. He did not describe her picking flowers but, like Rhea, weaving a robe of them over the earth. She was just embroidering the last element – a scorpion, the sting among the leaves – when she was taken. This happened in a high meadow in the mountain forests, like his own wandering places, and Pluto drove through it in a chariot pulled by dark-maned horses, putting out a grey hand to entice her to descend with him. It was the will of Fate, Orpheus sang, and the pattern of life, that the bright girl should descend into darkness. His Eurydice usually preserved both these aspects: the frivolous surface, the solemn depths. All depended on how he looked at her, how he loved her, how he sang her into life.

Certain medieval Eurydices came close to Persephone's character. Her name was traced to *Eur-dike*, 'deep judgement', and she too was often a queen, listening to Orpheus as he played his troubadour songs beneath her window (crowned with flowers, his long sleeves trailing), or summoning him to play as the plates were taken up at supper. In Robert Henryson's version of the story she was the Queen of Thrace, so powerful that she could command Orpheus wordlessly, 'with blenkis amorous', to marry her.

Remigius of Auxerre in the ninth century made her Music itself, the underlying meaning of the songs Orpheus sang. Behind the lattice or among the maze-hedges of the garden, she occasionally allowed him to see her. But she could never be considered his. She was the beautiful theory, which he, as 'divine eloquence', attempted to express in clumsy, sensual notes; she was the ultimate source of his knowledge, extending beyond Nature into the hidden realms of the dead. Music was only one name for her; Wisdom was another. Francis Bacon assumed she was natural philosophy. In essence she was Mystery, neither named nor understood. Rilke saw her as the 'number-less, inexhaustible' rose into which Orpheus led him, singing the secret interlayering of petals that became, as he explored them, increasingly deep-scented, naked, scalloped, soft:

> In your abundance like layer on layer of garments
> round a body made only of light.

There would be bliss in that unveiling. But if he neglected to attend her she would abandon him, her abundance withdrawn and her light shuttered. Her petals, dropping gently, would reveal nothing. Whether Music or Wisdom, Mystery or Beauty, she would vanish from his life because he had never really named or possessed her.

Supposedly Orpheus loved Eurydice more than any mortal has ever loved. Romans and Elizabethans alike made him the quintessential love poet, an amorous shepherd in his pastoral of flowing brooks and shaded bowers. Yet he was seldom described as falling in love like other men. How this passion had begun was unnecessary to the story. Only Jean Anouilh made anything of their first encounter, a glance across the dingy buffet of a railway station, where 'if only a bird had flown overhead, or a child had cried', their eyes might never have met, and they might have boarded separate trains. Within moments they were standing close, transfixed by each other, 'with everything that's going to happen to us lined up behind us'; within an hour, Orpheus had kissed her. Already, he loved her to distraction. He felt he had known her always; yet she quietly reminded him that in her changeability and mystery, like the rose, he had yet to discover who she was.

Elsewhere, he seemed to have observed the process from afar. The Orpheus of Apollonius's *Argonautica* had seen Eros at work in the palace of King Aietes, a swift-winged boy stringing his bow under the lintel of the porch. Eros had shot at Medea and then, laughing loudly, had flashed back to his perch among the roof-beams in the hall. Medea loved Jason after that; she could not do otherwise. The fire in her glances was under-stood even by the virginal lyre-player who sat apart, among the sun-flecked vines and the king's viscous fountains of milk and golden oil, tuning and dreaming.

The Neoplatonists, interpreting him later, made sure he intellectualised Love after their fashion. Love was 'posterior to the beautiful, but prior to every nature endued with love'; Love descended from intelligible natures to mundane ones, and called all things upwards to divine Beauty; Love bound mortals both to daemons and to gods. Orpheus's own hymns made it very much simpler: 'With your reins, you have harnessed the world.' In a tiny scrap quoted by Proclus he imagined the beginning of things, when Phanes

> cherished in his heart swift, sightless Love,

so that Love became the first-created: 'the oldest of all, first-born perfection, infinite Wisdom'. Round that mystery, all things came into being in the world. Aphrodite, goddess of love, gave her name in his calendar to sowing time, when seed was scattered prodigally over the waiting fields. Her marriage to Hephaistos, the lame artificer of the universe, meant that everything he crafted was also suffused with beauty and desire. When she was tired of Hephaistos she lay with young Adonis, coupling with him everywhere: on the sighing grass, by the embracing trees, among the kissing, mingling monads of the air, beside water woven endlessly with caressing, tender light. All Nature, Orpheus sang, was endlessly made by making love.

The two great gifts of the Greeks to humanity, said the poet Hölderlin, were Orpheus-Love and Homer-Song. But Love did not rule alone in Orpheus's universe, the ultimate controller of creation. It was everywhere bound up with Fate, Destiny, Necessity – or, as he sang of it, *moira*, the moving and breathing of divine Mind in 'all the things that are'. As Rilke wrote once, 'Fate does not come to us from outside: it goes forth from within us.' Like Love; like song.

So he did not court Eurydice, as far as anyone imagined. Ovid's Orpheus knew well enough what girls liked: 'shells and polished pebbles, little birds, flowers of every colour, lilies and painted balls, drops of amber that fall from poplar trees', and golden globes that bounced across the sand. He could make these globes leap skywards by themselves, form strings in the air, float off from a fingertip, as though he was a juggler at a fair. But there was no need for tricks or presents, since he could persuade Eurydice as easily as he lured the birch, the elm, the chestnut and the pine to follow him. Or Rilke's Vera:

> Dancer you were who, with limbs full of lingering, halted
> – as though of a sudden your young flesh was poured into
>   bronze –
> grieving and listening –. Then, from the high dominions,
> music fell into your heart, like a singing of swans . . .

There was a marriage of sorts. Monteverdi in 1607 imagined it best: nymphs springing from the mountains, shepherds dancing, and the smooth choral invocation of Hymen, god of marriage, to a temple on the wooded shore. As Orpheus sang of his happiness to the court of Mantua, resplendent in a feathered hat and slashed, figured velvet, all around him recorders trilled and sang like birds. But Ovid had witnessed a far grimmer ceremony. It took place without preliminaries or words on a chilly Thracian beach, with a grey surf breaking. The marriage – Roman in Ovid's imaginings – was doomed from its beginnings. Orpheus summoned saffron-robed Hymen, who came flying with his torch; but it smoked and could not be made to blaze with the necessary clear, pure flame, though the god stood tossing it, trying to ignite it, with fury and gloom on his face. There were no songs, either. Hymen refused to sing. Over the wedding table grey silence webbed the salvers and bowls, the knives and filigree vases, the little candy-saucers and the dusty apples, as if the wrinkled Fates had spread it there. Eurydice's robes were ash-coloured rather than saffron or flame, and when Orpheus carried her across the threshold, as Roman bridegrooms were required to do, she too was light as cobwebs and dust. She was already a shade, anticipating death. *Puella moritura*, Virgil called her: a girl bound to die.

They were husband and wife for only the shortest time, clinging together among shepherd tribes at the edge of the sea. Often they were seen as a couple alone against the world, privately and mutually absorbed, gazing at each other while hours ticked, travellers passed, meals were brought and ignored, lamps lit and doused again. Almost no one imagined a domestic scene for them. Anouilh set their brief love where travelling players belonged: in a dusty bedroom, shrouded with faux-velvet curtains, in a seedy provincial hotel. The only furniture was a huge iron-framed bed on which they lay awkwardly in their clothes. But then Orpheus was hardly ever within four walls, or even on a chair.

Apart from medieval Orpheus, in his castle of turrets and towers, only Cocteau's Orpheus was allowed a home, a restored farmhouse on a long, straight road somewhere in the suburbs of Paris. It was fitted up in best bourgeois taste with loud wallpaper, heavy tablecloths and the latest appliances. Busts of Greek gods graced the mantelpiece; statues stood by the garage. In this *ménage modèle* Orpheus led a life of sober celebrity until he fell in love a second time; in love with his own Death.

He knew her only as the Princess, pale, severe and beautiful. He had glimpsed her outside the Café des Poètes and followed her through the markets and arcades of the city, where she occasionally allowed him to see her. She symbolised, Cocteau wrote, 'that deep affection poets have for everything that goes beyond the world they live in'. Eurydice, 'impermeable to mystery' but too sensible to feeling, with her silk housecoats and neatly permed blonde hair, watched in fearful bewilderment as her husband drifted away: irritable, obsessive, taking to drink when he had never drunk before. ('*Je bois, ça te dérange?*') And at night they slept in separate, small beds.

Indeed, it was never certain that they slept together. In some versions of the story Eurydice was poisoned as she ran from the temple into the meadows, leading the wedding dance. She remained, like Persephone, both married and virgin. And Orpheus remained, as he was often imagined, edgy and abstracted: wrapped up in his music, following his own rules, so picky about food that he lived for days on wild plums and sorrel, grabbed from the stalk as he passed. Perhaps, like Pythagoras later, he refused to clean his teeth with oak or cypress wood, have his hair cut on feast days, or wear a ring with an image of a god, in case it picked up dirt from somewhere. Perhaps he cultivated silence ('control of the tongue'), and lay awake each morning rigidly beside her, trying to remember and monitor everything that had happened the day before. Perhaps, as Carol Ann Duffy saw them, he held her trapped 'in his images, metaphors, similes, / octaves and sextets, quatrains and couplets, / elegies, limericks, villanelles, / histories, myths':

the kind of a man
who follows her round
writing poems,
hovers about
while she reads them,
calls her His Muse,
and once sulked for a night and a day
because she remarked on his weakness for abstract nouns.

Perhaps most hurtfully he talked in riddles to her, laughing bafflingly afterwards, because he dealt in secrets, and she was only a girl.

Medieval poets, however, were sure they knew 'the sallies and sports of love', and Orpheus's own hymn to Aphrodite sang of the goddess's 'maddening love-charms' and her delight in the soft night-long couplings of lovers:

O sweet Persuasion, joying in love's bed,
moving in secret as your grace is shed,
Visible and invisible . . .

Earthly love was not supposed to be what Orpheus meant, here or anywhere. As Proclus insisted, he was singing of the replication in the lower realms of intelligible harmony and beauty, and of the procession of forms. He was never a sexual being, rather the reverse; creatures with high, hard cocks became impotent under his spell. At the Dionysian rites he was never pictured coupling with Maenads, riding or being ridden, though sexual arousal was part of completely becoming the god. Ostensibly he was dedicated to purity, as he was to solitude. But Clement of Alexandria, for one, was not persuaded. This 'theology' was full of sex-talk. Orpheus, he reminded his readers, had also paraded the ritual phallus when the wine god was worshipped, blatantly and joyously. And among the clutter in his 'mystic chests', Clement added, was a woman's comb, 'which is a euphemism and mystic expression for a woman's secret parts'.

Ovid, too, heard Orpheus sing of girls driven wild by passion: of Myrrha, in love with her father, kept awake by desire, running through the dark, climbing to the piled silk cushions of his bed: ashamed and yet eager, fearful and yet joyous, dreading the act and nonetheless wanting it more than any other thing. He also sang beautifully of female bodies: of the breasts of Pygmalion's statue softening and warming under the sculptor's hands (her veins throbbing, like lyre-strings, when his thumb pressed gently), or the glowing skin and flashing garters of Atalanta running.

Whatever occurred with Eurydice, he soon left her, as usual, to follow his higher calling: to sing in the woods.

*

Camille Corot saw him there. Down by the river at Ville d'Avray, just west of Paris, where the poplars thinned and their leaves quivered, green-grey, grey-white, blue-green, quicker than his dipping brush could follow them, he glimpsed the poet walking. He was taking long, determined strides, holding his lyre in front of him. The morning wind – the same wind that blew the willows silver-glinting, pale-green, sea-green, calling all the time for dashes and strikes of white –

billowed in his cloak and roughed his hair. Corot painted him
for the Paris salon of 1861 and again, better, for the salon of
1862, since so many viewers gave him their opinions on
Orpheus's pose, the clothes, the light. He knew, however, what
he was doing. He met him often.

At the edge of the woods he saw Orpheus once, where the
trees thinned out into meadows, just by the hedge. A lioness
had crept to lie down before him, listening, and a lion stood
entranced at a distance. Light strokes of charcoal caught his
notes, or cirrus clouds, disappearing over the hills. In 1865
Corot caught him on the verge of dancing, wrapped in a winter
cloak at dawn, almost overwhelmed by the massy shadow of
a tree that still carried night inside it. He was raising his arms
and his lyre to greet the sun. Corot sketched him in fine charcoal on brownish paper, darkest forms first, dispensing with
colours because he already knew them, avoiding any single
point of luminosity (though that point was vital to a picture,
whether in cloud, or face, or tree) because light filled the
whole sky on which Orpheus gazed.

On several mornings Corot waited for him early. Fuelled
only with strong coffee, his painter's smock pulled on over
his broad peasant head, he crammed paints and easel into a
knapsack and strode into the still-dark, silent woods. There,
settling his hefty frame under a tree, he let the scene become
magically ready for Orpheus, if he came.

'You don't see much at first,' he wrote to a friend:

Nature is like a white canvas on which some masses of
forms are vaguely sketched; everything is misty, everything
shivers in the cool breath of dawn. The damp, sweet smell

of the incense of Spring is in the air – you breathe deeply – a sense of religious emotion sweeps over you – you close your eyes an instant in a prayer of thankfulness that you are alive.

That whiff of incense sometimes announced him. Corot sat straighter, alert for the crunch of a sandal on the path, the snag of a cloak on brambles. For him:

Something is about to happen – you grow expectant, you wait, you listen, you hold your breath – everything trembles with a delight that is half pain:

At any corner of the scene Orpheus might step out again, smiling, lift his lyre, pluck it –

Bing! A ray of pale yellow light shoots from horizon to zenith... The dawn does not come all at once, it steals upon you by leaps and subtle strides . . .

Bing! Another ray, and the first one is suffusing itself across an arc of the purple sky.

Bing, bing! The east is all aglow.

The sun had risen. Orpheus was there on the path. And Corot, as one critic said, was 'painting for painting's sake, as the sun shines and the birds sing.'

*

Eurydice was left alone. There was no intimation of danger. No pricking thorn, no drop of blood pressed, in surprise, from a finger. Yet since that swift, savage attack on Persephone among the flowers, the risks were known.

Virgil's Eurydice was alone in a wild place – or playing, some said, with the nymphs beside the stream – when the bee-keeper Aristaeus ran after her and tried to rape her. He offered sweet, swift, uncomplicated pleasure, like drops of honey from the comb. Eurydice fled so fast that she did not see the serpent in the grass. (Virgil said it was a water-snake, a ripple in the stream and a thin, narrow head above the surface.) Or, picking flowers alone – for there was perhaps no Aristaeus, no rape, just the sunlight on fields at the forest's edge – she was bitten as she strayed. Wild hyacinth, white jonquil, red clover with its nibble of honey, yellow bird's-foot trefoil, made a path where her husband had passed and sung to them, a wreath for his dark hair. The narcissus of mortality once more lifted up its too-sweet fragrance to her. So too did the wild strawberry, a tiny pip of sweetness no bigger than the puncture-wound on her ankle bone that suddenly breaks, wells with blood and screams Death, death, death.

The snake might have been Orpheus's familiar. Gods constantly took this shape in his theogony, slithering into knots to mate with, or escape from, each other. Time itself, the very beginning, lay in coils with its scales glistening, though there was then no light. Snakes slid out from rocks or down trees as he played, their evil neutralised by music. In the circles of time, he taught, the soul of a man – having entered a horse, a bird, a dog – became one of 'the race of cold snakes that creep upon the earth'. Its grey length rose up as Eurydice passed. Cold, tight, bright as a bangle, it twined itself around her. One note struck inside her the chill of the concealing stone, and the damp of the grass that grew too deep to be warmed or dried by the sun. It entered her bones. She tottered and fell, crying. The faint, high, continuing note drew Orpheus running from the woods. But there was nothing to be done.

Apollonius of Tyana said the poet knew songs that could raise the dead. Desperately watching once at the sickbed of a friend, he had racked his brain to remember 'some melody of Orpheus' that might have kept the man alive. Orpheus himself, his throat almost closed with panic, would have turned over prayers, spells, laments, incantations, to find the right warming, reviving notes. In the end, abandoning the lyre, pushing the sweat-damp hair from Eurydice's face, he could have forced his singing breath directly into her cold, stiffening lips, her sealed ears. But all his desperate songs could not revive her. He had called her into life, but could not now call her a second time; he could make sticks and stones jump up and dance, but not the girl he had barely had time to call his wife.

Monteverdi's Orpheus heard the news from a dryad messenger. He fell mute as a stone. All he could muster was *Ohime*, 'Alas': two bleak notes, G sliding to F sharp. As the blood had drained out of Eurydice, so music drained out of him. When he tried to sing again it was in different, jarring tonalities, the words aching to a stop, as though his breath had gone. All the harmonies of the scene were shattered. For some long moments, he died with her.

Medieval moralists told a different story. In her long green robes, wimpled in white silk, Queen Eurydice wandered heedlessly in a garden of delights. She went 'to tak the dewe and se the flowris spring', said Henryson: quiet pleasures. In this guise she was a creature of the senses again, Affection, Passion or Desire; Orpheus was Intellect, the higher self. He had tried, like any good husband, to keep her in order: 'tuning', as he called it, or returning the mind to its proper tone, like a lyre. But she had merely laughed at him and run out into the sun.

The neat, clipped bushes were heavy with star-shaped flowers, signs of worldly temptation. Eurydice bent her smiling head towards them, one fair plait falling from beneath her veil. With her long white fingers she picked three blooms and tucked them between her breasts. From his palace Orpheus watched her and, despite himself, loved her, his lower, undisciplined self.

She was barefoot. Desire roamed the earth naked, or at least unshod, and delighted to feel directly the cushioning sand and the cool of the grass. This sensuality was her downfall. For there in the grass lay Worldly Deceit, or the Devil himself, covered in spots or scales, with a curling tail and stumps of legs bearing long, raking claws. He seemed quiet, couchant: an armorial beast, perhaps, carved out of harmless stone. But his mastiff's head and rough, licking tongue hid teeth, sharp Sin, that in a trice would kill her.

This Eurydice was almost Eve, but she had picked no apple of knowledge from the tree. She was too spiritually slothful even for that. Nonetheless, disaster had to follow from her carelessness. In *Sir Orfeo*, under a red-and-gold-globed apple tree, Queen Heurodis lay down heedlessly and slept in the heat of noon, the dangerous 'underentyde'. Fairies lurked there, as under all dream trees, to entrap young women at that warm hour of day; she did not see them, or the filmy dragonfly gleam of their wings among the leaves. The King of the Fairies rode past then, with a hundred knights and a hundred damsels on snow-white steeds, in milk-white clothes; on his head was a crown of a single gem, which shone like the sun. Politely but firmly, he seized Heurodis and took her to the other side.

At first she was returned, wild and speechless with horror, tearing her face and her fine clothes. Sir Orfeo, distraught, stood by her bed, holding the small pale hand on which blood was drying on the fingers and beneath the nails, and pledged that if she was seized again, he would go with her. The next day he sat under the tree beside her, ringed round with his knights. But still she was abducted.

In Henryson's poem it was Persephone, the Queen of the Fairies, invisible and unrelenting, who swept her to the land of the dead. In either case she was simply in a deep swoon, though the heart of Henryson's Eurydice was 'reft in pecis small' by the snake-bite. But whether dead or alive, she had been 'taken'; and she had vanished definitively from the upper world.

Orpheus mourned her for seven years. He raised a marble tomb by the side of Lake Avernus, one of the entries to the Underworld. It stood in a grove of dark laurels and cypresses, to which nymphs and shepherds brought memorial garlands of myrtle and scented flowers.

In 1762 Christoph Gluck, writing his *Orfeo*, heard him crying there, 'as if someone was sawing through his bones'. He cried 'Eurydice! Eurydice!' as though she could be found there, among the mute memorials. Against the funeral hymn of the mourners, moving in quiet diminished intervals, his agony seared the heart. But only Echo, in the reedy, distant oboe, deigned to answer him:

Ma sola al mio dolor
L'eco risponde.

It seemed to Gluck, though, that Orpheus was trying to keep his pain in check. He sang in the pure, detached manner of the *alto castrato*, the sparest mode imaginable: light and high, as he had sung in the forests long ago. Every gesture was 'full of grace and propriety', simple and unaffected. There were no tricks here. No cadenzas, *ritornelli* or 'barbaric extravagances' coloured his song; he followed the natural modulations of his grief. Just a little *portamento*, with rising swell and dying fall, shaped what he sang, 'like the dying notes of an Aeolian harp'. The technique was ancient, but also shockingly new in the opera of the time. Nor was Orpheus in the powdered wig and buckled shoes of operatic fashion, but in a plain long Grecian robe, as in the past.

Calzabigi, Gluck's librettist, was similarly struck by the pathos of the scene. 'All is nature here, all is passion,' he wrote in 1767 to Prince Kaunitz, Austria's chancellor of state:

There are no sententious reflections, no philosophy or politics, no paragons of virtue . . . the music has no other function than to express what arises from the words, which are therefore neither smothered by notes nor used to lengthen the spectacle unduly, because it is ridiculous to prolong the sentence 'I love you' (for instance) with a hundred notes when nature has restricted it to three.

Indeed, 'I love you' was all Orpheus wished to say; beside Eurydice's tomb, or in any other place. Virgil was closest to him as he lingered, 'sick to the heart', singing to the soul-bearing winds at the edge of the monotone sea:

> You, sweet wife, he sang alone on the lonely shore,
> You at the dawn of day, you at its end –
>
> *Te veniente die, te decedente canabat.*

Rilke, encountering him at this stage in 1906, thought a whole world of sadness was created now by his music: a nostalgia world of the wood, the dale, the path, the hamlet, the river, where he had loved her:

> and round this complaint-world, just the same
> as round the other earth, there was a sun
> revolving and a quiet starry sky,
> complaint sky with distorted stars –

Henryson's Orpheus wept too in this disordered world, and his lyre wept with him, 'thy golden pynnis with thi teris weit'. His grief so moved the woods that birds began to sing around him and the trees to dance 'with thar leves grene', as if they could comfort him. But nothing could. *Sir Orfeo* went to the city, where in every street he cried out Eurydice's name, desperate to recover her. He was reduced to love, and defined by it; there was nothing else. He appointed his steward to look after his kingdom, made provision for parliament to be summoned. Then, alone, he strode off to the wildwood.

He wandered there barefoot, hatless, in rough russet, with his harp slung on his back. Henryson said he made his

bed with 'bever, brock and bair'. In *Sir Orfeo* he became a
hermit, bedding down on the hard, springy heather, wrapping himself in grass and leaves. Where attendants had
snapped to his every need, now only 'wilde wormes' slid
past him. His food was roots and berries; he became lean,
and his skin withered with hunger. A long, rank beard grew
down to his belt. His beloved harp he hid in a hollow tree,
taking it out to play only when 'the weather was clear' –
which, on those cold northern moors, it seldom was. At
warm noontide he would often see the fairy king with his
grim armed retinue, Eurydice's abductors, riding past to
lance his heart again:

> Come to hunt him al about
> With dim cri & bloweing.

Traditionally he also moved the high Rhodopes to cry with
him. They had come to him before, together with towering
Athos, shattering their crags as they heaved forward. The snow
had melted from their flanks as his music crept inside them.
Now he sent it again, pushing deeper and fiercer under the
pressure of his tears. The hard maze of calcite grains began
to slide and move like a river, bearing down glassy flakes of
mica, shards of black graphite, bumping spheres of quartz.
Scarred passageways of ancient fire broke open under his
bleeding, thrusting notes. Inside the limestone folds of Pindus
a calcified forest began to stir like living trees, stone coral to
sway as though the sea still surrounded it. The mountain's own
song had become the alternate drag and spasm of his tears.
And that alone made the dead earth move and ravines crack
open with a deafening roar, until men saw the humped-up

horizon shift towards the sea, and the first slow-rolling boulders hurtle into the deep, still blue.

He searched wide Heaven too, by several accounts. Thracian shamans had no fear of flying. He murmured to Rilke, as they both watched an aeroplane circling, that a man 'must *be* the far-offness he flies'. He could gaze down on Earth from there, spiralled with the dark-blue sea. And this voyage was also internal; for the farthest sphere of the universe was also mirrored in him. Henryson saw him soar up by way of 'Watling Street', or the Milky Way, to the circular houses of the seven spheres. Each planetary god, from cold Saturn to swift Mercury, was beseeched with formal obeisances to tell him where Eurydice was, or to help him find her. Apollo was asked to take pity on 'thi barne and child' by lending Orpheus his shining face and not allowing clouds, or darkness, ever to obscure his search for her. He petitioned Venus especially, the loyalest of lovers as he called himself, on his knees in that soft, bright, arousing light. Yet all he brought back was the music of the rolling spheres, heavenly harmony skirling like organ pipes in the emptiness of space. Heaven could not hold material things, or earthly love:

> Sir Orpheus, thou sekis all in vayn
> Thy wyf so hie; thar-for cum doun agayn.

He had failed both in the earth and above it. There was only one expedient left to try. It involved, as Monteverdi's Orpheus foresaw, an assignation with Death: for some brief time, or for ever. But he was not afraid. He could do this, as he could also turn back the silver rivers and persuade

the winds to drop. He would go down to Hell to recover
her.

> *A dio terra,*
> *a dio Cielo,*
> *e Sole a dio.*

Farewell Earth, farewell Heaven, and Sun, farewell.

Orphée, 1950

Fifth string: Death

He had never been more lonely; yet he did not go alone. Behind him to the mouth of Hades trailed poets, philosophers, theologians, psychologists, psychiatrists, cinematographers and composers. They crowded at the edge of the Stygian lake, notebooks open and pens ready for whatever he could tell them. Through the gloom came a flickering of mobile phones and a drift of long white coats.

Mythologists watched him enter as a seed falling: the ash-key turning in the wind, the kernel trodden underfoot, the grain flung out from the sower's hand. He sank into the earth until he released life. His husk rotted from him there, and white hairs of new roots crept out into the dark. A pale filament uncurled, like a question; the shoot grew. Orpheus, as a primitive god of vegetation, endured the cycle of the seasons from death to life, to death, to life again.

Freudians knew his journey as the slide into sleep, unconsciousness and dreams. From his bed, never disarranging sheets or pillow, he would find himself on a stone staircase, in a meadow of tall grass, in a familiar room. This was the world within, half-remembered, half-suppressed. It was made from faces barely glimpsed in the train, stories skimmed in the newspapers, deep and unspeakable desires. He would touch a leaf, half-draw a curtain, to be sure he had stepped over. The sense of touch would reassure him. Light was murky there, as if underwater; babies were articulate, old-faced and wise; the sea stood vertical, and purple cats appeared when the carpet was rolled back. Sexual obsessions lurked in the folds of the landscape, terror in the floral furnishings of a house, and the dark was the journey from the womb in reverse.

I have come to the borders of sleep, wrote Edward Thomas:

> The unfathomable deep
> Forest, where all must lose
> Their way, however straight
> Or winding, soon or late;
> They can not choose.
>
> . . .
>
> There is not any book
> Or face of dearest look
> That I would not turn from now
> To go into the unknown
> I must enter, and leave, alone,
> I know not how.

Mystics understood that journey. The path into darkness, silence or suffering was the *via negativa* through which God became apparent. The One could not be grasped, said Plotinus, until all images had been banished from the mind, all material things stripped away, even the self forgotten. Orpheus, making for the 'thrice-unknown darkness', was also Donne crying to God to batter his heart, Hopkins wrestling with his own barrenness, St John of the Cross entering the 'dark night of the soul' in which God lay hidden and unspeaking in an excess of light. Or Thomas, falling into a sleep that was also to become his death:

> The tall forest towers:
> Its cloudy foliage lowers
> Ahead, shelf above shelf:
> Its silence I hear and obey
> That I may lose my way
> And myself.

Carl Jung, as a child of three or four, followed Orpheus unwittingly in dream to a stone-lined, rectangular hole in a meadow at Laufen. Peering in, he saw a staircase leading down. Tremblingly, hesitantly, he descended to a great chamber containing a golden chair, where something like a fleshy tree trunk was enthroned in a nimbus of light. Only several decades later did he understand that he had entered an underground temple, the shrine of a God who was not to be named, represented by a ritual phallus. 'Through this childhood dream,' he wrote:

> I was initiated into the secrets of the earth. What happened then was a kind of burial . . . and many years were to pass before I came out again. Today I know that it happened in order to bring the greatest possible amount of light into the darkness. It was an initiation into the realms of darkness, and my intellectual life had its unconscious beginnings at that time.

Very much later, in 1915 when he was forty, he descended again. This time 'the spirit of the depths' commanded him to sink into himself. There he would find 'all the mysteries of

becoming and passing away'. His own *anima* led him inwards
– as Eurydice, in effect, led Orpheus. He was terrified, but
followed. 'Where are you leading me?' he asked. 'Into what
mist and darkness? Must I also learn to do without meaning?
What is there, when there is no meaning?' He understood
then that he must let 'the dark flood of chaos' flow over all
that was orderly in his thought or his life. Creation ran backwards, carrying him with it, day into night. Out of night –
as Orpheus too believed – would come new creation and initiation, though not without terror. The journey to Hell, Jung
wrote, 'means to become Hell itself.'

Throw away the lights, the definitions, Wallace Stevens
wrote, on the same path:

> And say of what you see in the dark
>
> That it is this or that it is that,
> But do not use the rotted names.
>
> How should you walk in that space and know
> Nothing of the madness of space,
>
> Nothing of its jocular procreations?
> Throw the lights away. Nothing must stand
>
> Between you and the shapes you take
> When the crust of shape has been destroyed.

Orpheus's own disciples knew this was his journey of initiation, when everything changed. Robed, his temples bound
with ribbons, his skin smeared with whitish gypsum so that he
had become a ghost himself, their teacher sat enthroned in a

clearing among the trees. Incense smoke drifted around him, white against Night's embrace. He seemed asleep. Exhausted with singing and with fighting demons, he had fallen into trance, his body inert but his mind already journeying deep into the realms of the dead. He would learn truths there, most of which could not be spoken. He would walk with spirits and gods, some terrifying and some offering an almost unbearable tenderness, beauty, intimacy: the welcome of a bride. He would find human souls, winged, naked and shivering, and lead them from bewilderment to brighter and surer ground.

Other routes could be tried. Orpheus could have gone to the cave of Trophonius in Boeotia, deep underground, pulled in feet-first through a body-tight tunnel with his offerings clutched to his chest, to learn the secrets of the cosmos and of other, future lives. But his own initiation involved a journey to the court of Persephone, who was Eurydice in her deepest guise: the keeper of the mysteries of the living and the dead. There all his questions would be answered.

Medieval theologians followed Orpheus into a lower world already licked by fire. As an enlightened soul – as Intellect itself – he had no business to be there, among small long-toothed devils and the crowds of the naked dead. He went only to rescue Eurydice, his lower self, with her blithe indifference to things divine. He went to redeem her from the darkness as he had once released her spirit from the tree, uniting her with him in the gold-rayed splendour of the endless love of God.

To the monk Beausire, writing in the fourteenth century, Orpheus was explicitly Christ. He went to harrow Hell to save Eurydice, who was all sinful humankind. Tenderly, He ripped her from the arms of the ruler of Hell; and as He led her to the upper world He sang out, in the words of Solomon, 'Arise my love, my fair one, and come away!'

Yet the journey was not so simple. Many medieval observers found Orpheus's motives more confused. Boethius, in his sixth-century *Consolations of Philosophy*, saw him tangled as he went in the snakes and briars of material longing, just as Eurydice had been. He could not free himself from earthly love, or from the body. He was still weighed down by the bonds of earth. That was why he ventured at all, on this so-called rescue; and that was why he could not hope to redeem a lower self still preening and flirting at the warm edge of Hell.

Psychologists watched Orpheus with more sympathy. His journey was the need to recover memories and retrieve what had been lost. A bundle of letters opened and reread ; a photograph album pulled from a drawer; a trip back to haunts of first love, in the hope of being happy. The looping handwriting speaks again, high and happy, of shopping, fine weather, walks with Mabel by the river, a slight chesty cough (but linctus settled it), in a stopped and different time. Like a pressed flower, the colour stays. In small, glossy prints Self and Eurydice stand by a door, or embrace by a hedge, squinting into ancient sunlight. In the same cold kiosk on the pier he sits for a while, with an oily paper of chips on his lap and the same seagulls swooping, bickering, edging along the rail. From there, as the PA system plays 'their' song, he may see the very hotel, just where it was. That was the room, two along from the corner, where someone else – though it cannot be someone else – has drawn back the curtain untidily and put a pair of trainers on the sill.

Perhaps, tentatively, he joins Facebook, posting her photo among the chatterers who knew her, both hoping and not hoping for an e-mail from her freckle-faced friend in Year 6, who will never grow older. Or (they would understand this in Orpheus's mountains) he puts up black-rimmed notices with her name and her photograph under the railway arch, in the bus shelter where the forest begins, on a wire fence that fronts a garden of withered runner-beans and sunflowers, trying to call to everyone's remembrance the slowly but inevitably departing soul. A paper of hairpins is touched, folded, shivered over; a leather glove is put on, smelled, flexed, for that faint perfume of the dead. Fate has decreed that these things should fade and decay. Free will, pushed by love, winds back the clock and believes it can start again.

From the dim recesses of the ninth century, Remigius of Auxerre tracked Orpheus also. He saw him entering the obscurity of his own thoughts to find Eurydice, the source and meaning of his art. He played as he went, curiously testing his notes against the darkness. By this he hoped to find her. A friend or lover, hoping to engage him, would have drawn no response. He was turned away, within, listening only to his own heart and where it might lead him.

Ten centuries later Guillaume Apollinaire saw Orpheus – a young man like himself, whether naked or in dandyish white suits – trailing a thin bright light into Hell. This was the artist's line, which would become the shape of his art. Orpheus was 'the voice of light' and, as he advanced, the silent dark split into colours, or notes, to receive him. The artist who followed him could bring out these colours, bright, vibrant, abstract, straight from his subconscious on to the canvas. Such 'luminous language' in paint, words or music was the purest form of art there was.

This journey of discovery had always been both solitary and dangerous. In the nineteenth century Orpheus was the poet, by compulsion and necessity alone, crossing a threshold and descending into himself. He might be essentially passive and receptive, full of Keats's 'Negative Capability': 'that is, when a man is capable of being in uncertainties, Mysteries, doubts, without any irritable straining after fact and reason'. Or he might be like Shelley, at the very end of his nerves, actively seeking to plumb the depths for 'truth'. The descent might destroy him. He might lose himself in the labyrinths through which his thoughts surged and poured, like an underground river. But this was the only path towards the deep wellspring of his poems, the divine source. In Shelley's words:

> Where is the love, beauty, and truth we seek,
> But in our mind?

This was the only way, too, to find the Beloved: a union not possible in the waking world, but only in some deep interior state. Eurydice now existed there, as if Orpheus had never yet known her.

Rilke already understood this journey. When Franz Xaver Kappus, a young poet, had written to him in 1902, wondering how to proceed with his writing, his advice had been uncompromising:

> You ask if your poems are good poems. You are asking me,
> but you will surely have asked others before me . . . and my

advice is that you should give all that up. You are looking outwards and that, above all, is what you should not be doing at this time. There is no one who can advise or who can aid you; no one. There is only one way. *You must go inside yourself.* You must seek for whatever it is that obliges you to write. You must discover if its roots reach down to the very depths of your heart.

Maurice Blanchot also knew that Orpheus had to go this deep, or deeper. Blanchot, writing in the 1940s, saw him enter the dark as a poet with two purposes. One was to rescue Eurydice, truth or art, and bring her into the light. But his second purpose was to look at her in 'the other night', as the still-unattained object of his desire. He wanted to see her as she was before he had recovered her, wrapped in her own darkness, all her beauty merely potential, like Night's beauty, waiting for him. Eurydice was 'the farthest that art can reach'.

In Cocteau's film, too, Orpheus was lured into a darkness he longed to understand. He went with an initiand's questions, most of them to do with death. His guide Heurtebise, a student who had breathed in gas to kill himself, already knew 'the secret of secrets'; the Princess, his own Death, naturally had 'all the explanations'. Orpheus was convinced that, as a poet, he had the right to know them.

Intimations had already reached him. Riding one day in the Princess's Rolls-Royce, lured towards the other side, he had heard strange, crackling phrases coming through the car radio. They were tapped out over short wave on a transmitter, like wartime code:

*Un seul verre d'eau éclaire le monde . . . deux fois . . . Attention,
écoute. Un seul verre d'eau éclaire le monde.*

A single glass of water lights the world . . . twice . . . Pay
attention, listen. A single glass of water lights the world.

For Orpheus, this was poetry. His own work had grown
stale; it had begun 'to stink of success, like a hung bird'. But
here in the radio was the wild originality he needed, sent from
'the divine night' out of which all inspiration came. Though
it sounded like nonsense, it also, surely, opened doors to the
other world of Death and of dreams.

*Le silence va plus vite à reculons . . . trois fois. Je répète: Le silence
va plus vite à reculons . . . trois fois.*

Silence goes faster backwards . . . three times. I repeat: silence
goes faster backwards . . . three times.

Les miroirs feraient bien de réfléchir davantage.
Mirrors would do well to reflect more.

He commandeered the Princess's car and sat inside it, day
after day, waiting to hear what the radio would say. It gave out
mere runs of numbers; ecstatically, he told Heurtebise that they
made his poems worthless. But Heurtebise knew better. True
poetry had to come from Orpheus himself, breathed out from
his own night, not drawn in from that other, divine night that
he was inclined to adore. 'Beware of Sirens,' Heurtebise told
him. 'Your voice is lovelier, be content with that.' Rather than
surrendering to the mysterious sounds that rippled round him,
Orpheus had to follow his own subconscious into his own dark.

There, he came slowly to understand, he would find what he sought: knowledge or art, beauty, or the meaning of the music he played. As he whispered into Rilke's ear, half-singing, half-breathing, descent was necessary.

> Only to him who dares take up the lyre
> even in the realm of the shades
> shall it be granted in awe to aspire
> to unendingly praise.
>
> Only one who has dwelt with the dead
> and tasted the poppy flower
> can be sure that the lightest, most delicate tone
> will not slip from his power.

It was also true that Orpheus went down to Hell because he loved; and he believed love was strong as death. But what exactly he loved, and who he went for, and whether Love and Death were different, was much less clear.

*

The way to the Underworld was well known. As Rilke had written, a few months before the visitation, the road lay wide open between life and death. And, he added, 'how close we are to knowing it':

> We, local and ephemeral as we are, are not for one moment
> contented in the world of time or confined within it; we keep
> on crossing over and over to our predecessors, to our descent,
> and to those who apparently come after us . . . Transitoriness
> is everywhere plunging into a deep being.

In Thrace each tumulus was understood to be an opening to the Underworld. At the entrance small vessels of perfume were ritually broken, or buried upside down. From there the shaman – Orpheus, if he had tried – could thrust into the central chamber through a long tunnel of stones. In the Rhodopes, though, they know he climbed down into an icy cave called the Devil's Throat, where the Trigradska river plunges underground in two great waterfalls, roaring into the dark. Thracians threw the bodies of their kings down there, to speed their journey to the land of the dead; for nothing that is fed to the torrent ever reappears. There was no iron-railed staircase in his day, descending for 300 steps through the thunderous spray among squeaking, circling bats. He clung, slipping, to the rocks beside the waterfall as the crack of daylight closed behind him.

On his voyage to Colchis he had passed another way in, a grim headland jutting into the Black Sea near the island of Thynias, where Apollo had walked in the dawn sky. There Acheron, the river of woe, debouched into the sea through a towering ravine. From the headland a narrow, rocky glen ran inland to a cave overhung by plane trees. Poisonous aconite grew there, yellow globes on sharp leaves, the fire-foam that had dripped from the jaws of Cerberus, the hound that guarded Hell. Perhaps Orpheus himself had scrambled down to the cave-mouth, or someone else had, to report that an icy wind blew out of it, frosting the inner walls, and that the sound of shivering leaves and shivering sea filled all the air around it.

He had also passed close to a third entrance: a cave beside the deep lake of Avernus, near modern Naples, where the gate stood open night and day. Many writers assumed he went to Hades that way. Trees rimmed the dark-blue water and, in the region round it, sulphur-breathing vents and gas flares littered the pumice-fields. As in Thrace, the sun struggled to shine through the foggy air. Living travellers to Hades via Avernus, Virgil wrote, were advised by the Sibyl to pluck a golden bough of mistletoe as a present for Persephone, to ensure they would return.

But Orpheus – by 'his own' account, as well as Virgil's – took a different route, passing through the gate at Taenarus, the deep gorge where he had prayed after disembarking from the *Argo*. The steep groves there were also hung with black, perpetual fog, as though some of the miasma of Hades was seeping to the upper world. Several days of prayer and sacrifice were required if he wished to enter. Presumably this was done, and he began the long climb down. No bough of mistletoe was needed. He would travel with his lyre alone.

Later writers imagined still stranger beginnings to his journey. Sir Orfeo in his hermit solitude saw sixty fairy ladies out hawking, white-robed on white horses. The face of one especially troubled him; it was Queen Heurodis herself. She glimpsed him too, and wept; her companions hustled her away. He trailed them, stumbling on foot, along a river, as his tears fell and the fairy falcons set up the water fowl. At last, the riders reached a rock and vanished inside it. He followed:

> In at a roche the leuedis rideth,
> & he after, & nought abideth.
> When he was in the roche y-go
> Wele thre mile, other mo,
> He com in-to a fair cuntray,
> As bright so sonne on somers day . . .

Cocteau's Orpheus had the simplest journey. He walked to the three-faced bedroom mirror and touched it with gloved, searching fingers to enter the other world. Mirrors, Heurtebise had told him, were 'the doors through which Death comes and goes'. It was even possible that all the mirrors of the world led to the other side. Rilke, writing Orpheus's words, seemed to agree: mirrors were 'openings in Time', *Zwischenräume der Zeit*, light-shafts in a forest of dim, empty rooms, whose true purpose no one knew. Unicorns came into being when mirrors were held up to them. So men might, too. As Orpheus pressed, the glass shattered softly around him. He passed into himself.

He had tried to go through before. In the Princess's Rolls-Royce he had been driven down a foggy road towards a level crossing that marked, perhaps, the course of Acheron, or the slow path of the Styx. 'The usual route,' she called it: *le chemin habituel*. Across the tracks the landscape had switched into negative, the fields snowy and the sky dark. Trees overtook them. They reached a chalet, or safe-house, in the woods. There the radio played music from Gluck's *Orfeo*, while Orpheus waited in dilapidated rooms. The Princess told him he was asleep; he suspected this was so, and that he inhabited a dream.

He knew it for certain when the Princess passed through a three-faced mirror in her bedroom, and he tried to follow her. Unsteady from the champagne she had given him, he pummelled the glass uselessly with his fists, and fell unconscious. He awoke elsewhere. A pool of water lay beside him, reflecting his dazed face; white dunes, baked in sunlight, rose up on the horizon. Heurtebise came in the Rolls-Royce and took him home. But on the second occasion, in his own bedroom with Heurtebise assisting, he stepped easily to the other side. He did not need to understand how it had happened, his guide told him. He needed only to believe.

What no one imagined was that he died, as death is ordinarily understood.

The basic geography of Hades he knew already. Dionysus and Heracles had journeyed there, among others. The meadows of Acheron and the 'misty lake' received all those who had lived purely under the sun; the impure went down to the plain of Cocytus and the dark pit of Tartarus. However she had behaved, Eurydice was now to be found there, in 'the vast hidden part of the earth'.

Generally, Hermes gave souls guidance in this place. Orpheus in his hymns described seeing him on 'the road of no return' beside Cocytus, fidgety and light-fingered, with his golden snake-wand and his snap-brim traveller's hat. The soul-bearing wind whistled loudly about him, as if he whistled himself. He would have eyed Orpheus's lyre with an inventor's grin, on tenterhooks to play. Or perhaps the two musician-magicians exchanged wry salutes, half-smiles at each other's skill and fortitude, before forging separate paths in the dark. Orpheus seemed to have no companion save his own hope or his own daemon, advising from within. Only Cocteau saw him accompanied by the sad, calm Heurtebise, assistant of the Death he loved. 'Breathe slowly and regularly,' Heurtebise advised him, in the play Cocteau wrote before the film:

'Don't be afraid; just walk straight ahead. Turn to the right, then to the left, then to the right, then go straight along. There, how can I explain it? There's no more direction . . .'

'And then?'

'Then? No one in the world can tell you. Death begins.'

Many imagined him almost naked there, the natural state of the human soul in Hell. Cocteau's Orpheus went casually dressed, in his poet's open-necked shirt. But the earliest portrayals of his journey, on Greek vases, showed him in the elaborate pleated and beaded robes of a citharode or professional lyre-layer, the clothes he had worn to sea. Ribbons hung from the seams and from his hair braids. They did not stir in the windless air, until he sang.

The 'usual route' in those times ran at first through fields. It forked constantly, to the right, to the left, as if in mockery of Orpheus's songs on the endless branching of life. The instructions he wrote later, based on his experience there, advised keeping to the right 'as far as you can go', through sacred groves and meadows and across the plain of Lethe, where the heat was brutal. Henryson made it a Scottish moor 'wyth thornis thik and scharp', which ripped his clothes. The landscape was one of dreams, continually shifting and changing under strange, filtered light.

He came at last to a meadow of lilies, a sea of pinkish-white petals stretching before him. This was the Field of Asphodel. On any ordinary day he would have paused to botanise, testing whether these familiar flowers with their tall bud-spikes, drooping stamens, thin grey leaves, were real, or would mist away under his touch. They surrounded him and brushed against him, ghost flowers. But Persephone's palace was already suggested by dark, distant poplar trees, as clumps of poplars on the Thracian plain marked the presence of unseen water; and at this point the path divided definitively, with one way going uphill to Elysium and the other down, steeply, to Tartarus. He could not linger here.

To the left of the road was a pool, with a white cypress leaning over it. This, Orpheus sang later, was the spring of Lethe, or Forgetting. On the right was another that poured ice-fresh from the Lake of Memory, where spirits guarded the water under weeping poplar trees. Pale winged shades crowded around the second spring, beseeching, rasping with thirst, for the cups handed out by the guardians. Later, he recalled their cries exactly:

> I am a child of Earth and starry Heaven;
> But my race is of Heaven alone, and you know it.
> I am parched with thirst and I perish. Give me quickly
> The cold water flowing forth from the Lake of Memory.

Those who drank from the first pool returned to earth through the punishments and purgings of the Underworld. Those who took the purifying cup of Memory were greeted gently ('Hail, thou who hast suffered the suffering'), and were destined for 'the seats of the holy' in the Heaven they now remembered. The hustling shades therefore claimed, constantly and clamorously, to be children of Heaven, though their shadow-voices made no more sound than the gibbering of bats. They moved like bats, too — those Orpheus knew from the caves and trees of his mountains — shifting as a mass in which one or two would always be falling and scrabbling back, wings half-lifting, trying to save themselves.

In his own case, though he was a sealed and initiated soul, he was told that he must drink from both springs: first from Lethe (one sip only, not like a Thracian), to ensure he would return to the world from Hades; and second from the Lake of Memory, to remember what he was about to see in the realms of the dead. Among the crying and resisting shades, jostling him with their faint limbs like branches in a wind – though there was, he recalled, no wind – he carefully carried out his instructions. The first sip brought 'the oblivion of the fallen mind', as he remembered it; the second was a brief but breath-cutting pang of beauty recalled, and pain.

From the place of the springs he took the road downhill. The way grew dimmer, but it was not yet terrible. 'His' hymn to the Fates described his first sighting of the Stygian pool that marked the western edge of Hades, 'the heavenly lake where waters white / Burst from a fountain hid in depths of night, / And through a dark and stony cavern glide, / A cave profound, invisible'. It then fell in silver whirlpools towards the sea. All his rivers were silver; this one, unusually, was silent. Nor was it visible to living men. But he was alive, the strange mingled waters still cool on his tongue, and saw it as beautiful with his shaman's eyes.

So he may have seen much of Hades. In his own theology it was neither dark nor dreadful, simply 'unseen' – the other side of life. His hymns called it 'distant, untiring, windless, impassive', words he used of divine regions. As a place of purification, where souls were freed from generation, it was 'better than the apparent', the gaudy world above.

Cocteau's Orpheus found a similar no-man's-land, made of 'the memories of men and the debris of their habits'. It was a realm of twilight, between life and death, with both landscape and observers wrapped in half-sleep, *une sorte de demi-sommeil*. Time did not exist there. Towering ruins filled the streets. To his still-living ears, each sound was amplified: the screech of machinery, the melancholy that echoed in the whistle of distant trains. A 'silent wind' buffeted Heurtebise, puffing out his shirt, blowing his oiled hair, but Orpheus could not feel it. 'There's no wind; why do you seem to fight it?' he asked Heurtebise. But the other side was not a place for questions. It was, as Rilke put it, 'beyond the why and the how'. Orpheus followed his guide, feeling his way in the dusk as though he swam. Human shadows lurked vaguely among the ruined walls. One shade alone became a person who passed close, turning as though he could not see them, with glass plates strapped to his back: a glazier, ready to work in a place where windows no longer mattered. '*Vitrier! Vitrier!*' he called, with infinite sadness.

'Are these people alive?' Orpheus asked.

'They think they are,' Heurtebise answered him.

*

Live music is not allowed here. At the foot of the escalator a notice makes it clear: play, and you'll be fined. The young man strides on anyway, into the labyrinths of Green Park Underground station, ostensibly towards the Jubilee Line, carrying his guitar.

Where the passage bends away to the left appears the perfect place. For a while the station-keepers will not find him here.

Both exits from the tunnel will be out of sight; no visible beginning, no certain end, but a long wall of curving blue-and-white tiles to echo to his sounds. His camp is simple: a folding chair, a Thermos of coffee, a blue blanket spread on the cold concrete floor, and the open, hopeful guitar-case. He swings the guitar from his shoulder, preparing to play.

His right hand grasps the plectrum; his sandal, dusty from the walk, beats time. He could not be more blatant. Each note strikes the walls like a sharp stone on metal, and amplifies as it progresses. His voice, high, sweet and clear, echoes back from the tiling that surrounds him. Long before you see him, and long after you have passed, the music tells you he is there; but at the moment of meeting it dips a little, as if his flesh and clothes absorb the hard edges of the notes he plays. Though he sounds like a master or a god, he is suddenly vulnerable then: just a man.

Ceaselessly the shades stream past. Their coats are grey, black or brown, death-colours. Rain soaks their shoulders, their hair, their half-furled umbrellas. Most look away from him and hug the walls, lured by the music and yet afraid to be complicit in it, or to give up something for it. A few stray closer to throw him coins, but still they will not meet his eye or speak to him. No human contact here. Their pre-paid cards have buzzed them through and the escalator has carried them down unmoving, wrapped in half-sleep, while the advertisements change around them. The world above is briefly forgotten here, the world below unfocused on. In the musty wind that blows along the passage they are swept like leaves, or huddling bats, to Canada Water or to Stanmore.

Customers are reminded to keep their luggage with them at all times.

Please stand well back from the platform edge.

The walls of the labyrinth are lined with posters for jewellery, hamburgers, lingerie, adventure films, dazzling tropical beaches where lips are about to meet. These are all part of the visible world the shades cannot leave behind. But from some other, unseen world comes the song that floats above the platforms, filtering like hope – or life – through the high mesh walkways and along the soot-caked pipes, before the next gusting wind from the tunnels carries it away.

*

Orpheus did not say how he charmed the Underworld's guardians to let him through. Others imagined it. To enchant Charon, the grizzled boatman who ferried souls across the Styx, Monteverdi's Orpheus summoned up all the daring of the music of the age. At the edge of the painted water, in feathered hat and velvets in the Stygian gloom, he launched into a highly ornamental song, vivid with coloratura. Each phrase was followed by glittering *ritornelli* for violin, cornet or harp, lightly echoing the beauty of his effortless twists and turns. He was showing the infernal spirits, as well as the gathered academy of Mantua, the very best he could do.

And he was deferential, as if Charon were the duke himself. He addressed him, though the boatman was old, bent and in rags, as *possente spirto e formidabil nume*, 'powerful spirit and dread deity', acknowledging who ruled on the fearful river. In his pauses, he gave courtier's bows. But Charon, in his stately, defiant bass, with a reed-organ moving in freezing chords behind him, remained unmoved. He had been tricked before, by Heracles and others. He was not fooled by Orpheus's politeness, or by the poignant melody the young man played on the lyre alone, or by his sheer bold anger in *recitativo*, the new style of 'speaking from the heart'. Orpheus tried all of them, his impatience increasing. He ended with anger:

> *Rendetemi il mio ben,*
> *Rendetemi il mio ben,*
> *Rendetemi il mio ben,*
> *Tartarei Numi!*

> Give me back my love,
> Deities of Tartarus!

Still Charon refused. Orpheus therefore knelt down, laying his hat beside him, and began to play as he had done in the sacred grove of Colchis, under the dragon-tree. The softest and holiest register of his lyre was now represented by *viola da braccio*, organ and *contrabasso* viols. Playing in this mode he lulled the old man asleep, stole his boat and slipped, still singing, like a swan, across the waters of Death.

> *Rendetemi il mio ben,*
> *Tartarei Numi!*

In the ancient writers, Charon never dozed. He went on working, implacable, his rheumy eyes two staring orbs of flame. But in the end he relented. He did not object to taking this passenger, though Orpheus weighed down his boat, making grey water well through the cracks in it, and pressed the required coin too strongly into his mildewed hand. The old boatman would have sensed, too, as music continued to weave and ring about him, that his pole was not needed to move the boat across the windless river. The Styx was suddenly webbing and foaming underneath him as the Hebrus did, curling into eddies and tight silver waves that shattered softly on the opposite shore. Charon was not allowed to transport the living, with or without their lyres. But he was suddenly powerless to do otherwise.

On the far bank the crowds of the dead stood pale as reeds. Orpheus later described them as 'beings made of dreams'. Leaping from the boat, he brushed through them – though in some accounts they welcomed him as an ambassador of Love, taking his warm hand in theirs. The hound Cerberus admitted him, lulled asleep as Charon was, or placid and drooling from three sets of jaws. Hell drowsed as he entered, as if it had already surrendered.

Later writers filled Hell with particular torments: Tantalus gasping soundlessly for unattainable water, Sisyphus pushing a huge rock that rolled inexorably downhill again, Ixion stretched on a noiseless wheel that pulled him taut as it turned. Orpheus himself did not describe these. But each soul he encountered longed, in his words, 'to cease from the cycle and gain breathing space from evil'. Each had found the punishment most fitted to itself.

The first torture he witnessed was on the banks of Cocytus, as it flowed 'mournfully' through the darkness. Here the un - initiated were buried to their necks in viscous, stinking mud.

This represented their sins, from which, after hundreds of years, the grey coiling river would absolve them. At another point in the journey a great jar stood half-buried beside the path. Tired men and women, old folk and pale, winged children were carrying pots of water towards it. The pots leaked; or they had smashed, and the shades balanced water in the broken shards. It dripped through their trembling fingers. These, he understood, were also the uninitiated; the pots and fragments symbolised their souls, imperfect and unsealed, uncontrollably spilling out material desires. They would go on bringing water, and losing it, until they had earned purification. He pitied them, and yet the Orpheus who had lost Eurydice knew his own soul was not yet free of desire. That was why he had come.

As he walked he may have let his lyre hang silent by his side. His own hymns told of wide, sad, twilight plains in Tartarus, where the agitated dead flickered hither and thither without rest and without breath. A song there would vanish into the immense mourning distance, as it did in his own Thracian grasslands. But Virgil thought he sang. Seneca imagined that the sound poured through like a river, Ovid that it rang out like a clear, pealing bell, pushing back the soundlessness of death. Virgil thought the place was forested, with suicides and sad lovers much like Orpheus haunting the myrtle groves, and that thousands of phantoms flocked to hear him, 'numerous as the birds that hide among the leaves when the evening star or a wintry shower drives them from the hills'. Music, which was life, and light, and love, shocked with its presence a place that knew none of those things.

Yet it was becoming harder to hear it. As he advanced, pine torches burst out of the dark again, and the overwhelming silence was sliced by long metallic screams. Both Gluck and Monteverdi filled the depths of Hell with pitiless brass. The Furies were unleashed to torment him, screeching in octaves as flames burst out of the clouds. Cornets and oboes, an *orribile sinfonia*, blared across the poet's gentle pizzicato strings. Yelling and jabbing at him, they demanded to know who he was. He tried to answer; they grabbed hold of him, clawing him like Maenads in the dark. Their bats' wings clattered round him; their faces were cracked and blackened, as though they had been burned. Snakes writhed in their hair. At a glance from their eyes his flesh began to blister and break open, though without blood, as though his life had dried. Horror rooted him to the spot, numbed his helpless arms to his sides. His mouth was open, but what came out of it was mostly soundless fear. They could impose this terror on him because, like the dead, he could see them. Music was no protection this time: they were music, too.

Shivering convulsively, he begged to go past. Snake hair hissed in his face, spitting out refusals. Blasts from the trombones, their shrieking throats, shattered against his words. Infernal music scraped, scratched and gouged him, like a thicket he could not leave. But this Hell was his; it was no one else's. *Ho con me l'inferno mio*, Gluck's Orpheus sang to his tormentors. They could do nothing worse to him. Since he had made this Hell, he could also prevail against it.

Desperately, singing unremittingly, he did so. Gradually, lyre and voice had their effect. The Furies' racketing wings beat more slowly. Their claws retracted, and the screaming brass lost its edge. Over their blackened brows the snakes began to droop and curl, charmed harmless.

They sank down at last, feeling his magic take hold in them. Unable to resist it, they let him through. His terror had subsided, and the gates were flung open before him. Ahead lay the palace of the rulers whose hearts 'knew not how to soften to human prayers'. He would try.

This was the most dangerous, the deepest point. Ovid and Virgil imagined him at the nadir of the infernal pit; Henryson saw him in 'a fereful strete', dark as night, with 'a stynk rycht odiouse' from a furnace full of burning kings, emperors, popes and archbishops, their mitres and hot brass crowns crammed into the flames. Czeslaw Milosz glimpsed him on a murky, benighted street in the city, hunched in his coat as headlights swept past. He hesitated to knock at the blank glass-panelled door.

But ancient painters saw Orpheus emerge from a grove of dim poplars that dropped amber tears. He arrived at a pleasant portico, with columns and carved pediment. From the ceiling of the inner hall hung wheels, his own symbol of life, death and rebirth. These gave the only indication of what this building was. Sir Orfeo, too, was dazzled by crystal walls and golden pillars that made the night sky glow. Only later did he notice the torn and tortured bodies of the dead or the 'taken' strewn casually, like rag dolls, around the palace. Under a red-and-gold-globed apple tree outside lay his own Queen Heurodis, asleep. He knew her by her clothes.

Some formal announcement was needed as he entered. Two

figures faced him; but he had eyes for one alone. Beside Hades, or Pluto, the pale King of Death, sat fair-haired Persephone, snatched so fast by Pluto from the upper world that earth-light still clung to her, like sunlit blades of grass. Orpheus's salutation was principally to her. Flickering torches and ears of wheat surrounded her, tokens of the earth-life she still determined and the secrets she knew. Violets, the death-flower, were twined in her hair. An apple was in her hand, sunset-coloured, picked – as he recognised – from the far-western tree by which he had once pleaded for water and for life.

In the earliest, ancient accounts of his descent, he went simply to commune with her. Love and Death were interchangeable. His love and his death were bound up utterly with her. She was the principal goddess whose rites he celebrated: she contained the moon and Wisdom, Artemis and Athena, his 'Goddess of Light', now an arm's length away. The willows along his rivers, their green screens shimmering with songs, were her trees, touched as tentatively as he might stroke her hair. He had spoken of her, dreamed of her, sung of her, but did not know her. His own hymn to her was full of contradictory praises, for she was a sum of opposites, like all his gods. Stammering like a lover, he would call her virgin, but also the mother-goddess of green fruit, new shoots and the flowers of spring; the dealer of life, as well as death; a heedless, meadow-roaming girl, but also the 'pure, pure Queen' of the world he had now come to, the unseen world below. In his later rites the new initiate was embraced by a priestess, representing her, and pressed his head like a child beneath her warm, full breasts. He spoke the words of the soul that had passed through punishment and was ready for rebirth; ready to leave.

I have sunk beneath the bosom of the Mistress, the Queen
 of the Underworld,
And now I come a suppliant to holy Persephone.

Orpheus's words were similar. There was more to the prayer,
but it was enough for the moment to murmur this much:
hoping for grace, already in bliss.

Cocteau's Orpheus had long been in love with her. He was
entranced by the Princess's elegant, pulled-back hair, her hard,
cruel mouth in which cigarettes trembled as she lit them, and
her knot of pearls, like a noose. With one snap of her long
gloves, she commanded silence; she demanded *une discipline
méticuleuse*, as on a ship. Her slim wrist held a watch that she
consulted obsessively, though time did not exist for her.
Orpheus had gone down to Hell to find her, his own Death,
as much as to retrieve his wife.

The Princess, in turn, loved him, although he had no idea
how much. Leather-clad motorcyclists, acting on her orders,
had killed Eurydice on the long, straight road outside their house
so that she might have him for herself. Silently, each night, she
would steal into his bedroom through the three-faced mirror
to watch him as he slept. Cloak and hood framed her white
face, like the moon above him. He dreamed her; she told him
that 'the role of the sleeper is to accept his dreams'. As a poet,
he needed to go through many encounters with her – many
deaths – before he could truly know rebirth; until, in Mallarmé's
words, he was 'changed at last into himself by eternity'.

But he could not stay for long in this enchantment. He had
to sing as he had never sung before. Even to speak, in this place,
was an ordeal. Ovid heard his first polite, necessary words:

O ye Gods and Powers immortal,
Rulers of the lower land!
No man living can avoid you.
None escapes your dread command.

Deep silence fell. Indeed, perhaps only Orpheus broke it; there was no reason why the gods should have replied to him. He straightened his back into the musician's pose, the lyre in his left hand, the plectrum in his right, and steadied his breathing. There was time for only the briefest tuning; the lyre held to his ear for a moment, then lowered again. Slowly, his sandalled foot began to beat time on the cold flagstones of Hell. Ancient vase-painters showed him swaying as he sang, his long robes rippling with the force of his words.

Ovid attempted to imagine what those were. His Orpheus was a standard performance poet, hobbled by nerves and good manners before the gods, as any mortal would be. As always, he stared heavenwards, not at them. And he began with excuses. He had not come, he explained, to see Tartarus, or to chain up Cerberus, or even to pay homage to the dark deities he addressed. He came because his wife was dead.

He described her death, 'young as she was'. His song slowed; this was difficult. He evoked her, just a girl, running in the grass, bitten by the snake. So gently, artlessly sung, the implosion of his life.

How could I bear that sorrow,
how restore what could not be?
I struggled to endure it,
but Love has conquered me.

Around him, Hell paused and listened. Ovid saw all movement stilled, all torments suspended. Jan Brueghel the elder
assembled an audience of the rapt and bizarre: lizards in red
nightcaps, armour-plated grasshoppers, moths with owls'
heads and, in the near distance, a bourgeois couple marooned
in a boat in the upper branches of a tree. Around Orpheus,
where they still hovered, the bat-winged Furies slobbered their
leather cheeks with tears.

He wondered aloud whether Pluto and Persephone knew
about love: what it was, how it felt. Certainly, he sang, Love
ruled in the upper world. Perhaps Pluto had felt something
like love when he snatched Persephone away, and she had
begun to sense its shadow when, dark weight looming from
darkness, he had started to kiss and embrace her.

But Orpheus dared not take the theme too far. He did not
know that any emotion was involved in their case, though
they sat with hands loosely linked, like lovers. The gods had
their own imperatives. He therefore changed tactics, no longer
assuming the powers of Hell could understand him at all.

> I implore you by these regions,
> by this Chaos, black as Night,
> by this silence (subject to you),
> weave her back into the light!

He did not mean for ever. Even in desperation, he knew
that he must check himself. He let the music restrain him, a
quiet coda. Just the loan of Eurydice for a while would be
enough. Of course, in the end the gods would take her again;
the inexorable laws must be obeyed. He accepted that.

They might not agree even to the loan, but then his course

— and theirs — was easy. They should take him too, because
he had no wish to live without her. The end of his song resolved
into a simple offer: Release her, or take me.

Ovid's Orpheus did not sing for long. He kept to the point,
no words wasted. Czeslaw Milosz heard something quite
different: neither diplomatic nor tactical, just a paean to life,
the most shocking thing imaginable at that time, in that place.

He sang the brightness of mornings and green rivers,
He sang of smoking water in the rose-coloured daybreaks,
Of colours: cinnabar, carmine, burnt sienna, blue,
Of the delight of swimming in the sea under marble cliffs . . .
Of the tastes of wine, olive oil, almonds, mustard, salt,
Of the flight of the swallow, the falcon,
Of a dignified flock of pelicans above a bay,
Of the scent of an armful of lilacs in summer rain,
Of having composed his words always against death
And of having made no rhyme in praise of nothingness.

That was truer than it seemed. He had never praised death
in so many words. He had sung life, in all its energy and
beauty; but death, for him, was unseen life.

Most writers left his song to the imagination. The effects spoke
for themselves: the Underworld stunned to immobility, or to
tears. One fifteenth-century poet heard Persephone cry out in
surprise, because the realm of Death had never heard love before.
Henryson said that the music of the spheres, that 'swete propor-
cion' brought back by Orpheus from the Heavens, so astonished
the courtiers that they lay down at his feet to listen.

Enthroned among them, the rulers wept. Milton saw 'Iron
tears' steal down Pluto's cheek. Persephone, feeling the ache

and sting of human love, softened at once. She agreed to give Orpheus what he desired. But Pluto recalled 'the immutable law'. He made one near-impossible condition if Eurydice was to be restored to him: that Orpheus could not look at her until he was once more across Avernus, in the upper world, lit by the sun.

From among the shades, Eurydice was brought forward. She was pale, limping from her unhealed wound, in her grey grave-and-wedding clothes. Or she was shining, heart-stopping, though still veiled: the Beloved, or secret Wisdom, suddenly vouchsafed to him. In any event, he did not see her. He had turned immediately away.

They seemed allowed to talk, but in no case did he explain. Often her hand was placed in his, like a plectrum or a stone. They touched, but did not connect. On this long walk they were not one, but two; the longed-for union had not yet occurred. In the distant light she would be his again, one completing the other. But for the while, as Anouilh's Orpheus cried, they were in the unbearable state of being two: 'each of us on our own, quite shut in . . . two prisoners, each tapping on the wall from the depth of his cell'. Many versions did not even place them close as they walked from Hell. In ancient depictions Eurydice's guide was often Hermes, the guardian of transmigrating souls, while Orpheus strode ahead of them.

But who, or what, did he lead out of the depths? Perhaps his own sensual self, passion spent and tears dried: penitent, subdued for a while, but then suddenly fretful, scared among the looming defiles and on the vertiginous bridges, venting little exclamations of misery and pain. Once again, as in the old days, she soon became disorderly and demanding. Gluck's Eurydice, dawdling and hurt, could not understand why he would not look at her, hold her, kiss her. '*Vieni! Segui mi passi!*' ('Just follow me!') he snapped in reply. Anouilh's Eurydice told him she felt too weak, too 'feeble and flickering', to be worth this awful journey. She would only disappoint him, because he was 'terrible as the angels' and she was just an ordinary girl, wanting to live.

But perhaps he did not lead out that fragile, plaintive Eurydice at all. Perhaps this was the other *Eur-dike*, deep Truth or deep Wisdom: his mystic bride, or the revelation drawn from Persephone herself, or the art born out of mystery and darkness. She was slippered and uninjured, bathed in serenity, but reluctant to oblige him. If he quickened his pace, impatient, she merely fell further behind him. To take her hand would have been an outrage; it was she who directed him. Since he could not make beautiful music without her, since his mystical insights depended on her, he had to rest whenever she did, respecting the arrangement. He was mute and trembling at what he had found and what he had been allowed to do.

Here he had to behave like a man in deep study, who is suddenly aware that he has hooked something; but rather than tug on that line within himself, rather than confront what he is frightened to contemplate and more afraid to lose, he gets up, makes a mug of coffee, uselessly sorts a pile of papers, and goes to the window to gaze intently at the grey roofs or the trees.

'Why', cried Coleridge once, 'do I always turn away from any interesting Thought to do something uninteresting?' He had been struck, on a December night in 1803, by the reflection of his study fire in the window, a metaphor perhaps for the soul within the body, but as soon as the thought struck him, 'I turned off my attention suddenly, and went to look for the Wolff I had missed – Is it a cowardice of all deep Feeling, even tho' pleasurable? or is it laziness? or is it some thing less obvious than either?'

In any case, Orpheus walked softly, as a man must who suddenly knows for certain that he is in a dream.

It was on the journey out that Rilke had first met them, a frail figure in suit and Homburg stepping from the shadows. The date outside was 1906, with the garish flowers of a Roman spring beyond his window. There was no date within. He was in the meadows of Hades, beside 'the pale strip of the single pathway / like a long line of linen laid to bleach'. Orpheus as Rilke glimpsed him, slender in his blue cloak, was neither playing the lyre nor singing. Instead he was striding ahead with clenched fists, tense and silent. Behind him trailed Eurydice, with Hermes guiding her. Rilke noticed that 'the dead's long linen bands' were hampering her, preventing her from keeping up. But this was not the only reason for the acute sense of distance between them.

> She was within herself. Her having died
> filled her like fullness.
> And as a fruit is filled with sweetness and with darkness,
> thus she was full of her great death
> which was so new that she grasped nothing . . .

She was no more that fair-haired woman
who sometimes echoed in the poet's songs,
no more the wide bed's scent and island,
and that man's property no more.
She was already loosened like long hair,
given away like fallen rain,
distributed like hundredfold provision.

She was already root.

Eurydice had embraced her Death. Just as she had never wished to waken into existence, so she had no interest in returning there. As medieval writers understood, she was now Wisdom, inhabiting a deeper state and poured out into deeper being. If Orpheus truly wished to bring her back, mortal impatience would get him nowhere.

At the edge of the Styx she presumably caught up with him, her breath gentle on his neck. He stepped into the boat; it dipped a second time after him, but he did not turn to help her. The astonished boatman picked up his pole. Orpheus was aware, perhaps, of what might have been a bundle of light moss behind him. Rilke thought he heard nothing; she was too weak, too soft. The drip of water in the infernal caverns drowned any slight sound she might have made. Her husband was glad not to hear, not to know.

After the river the way was steep. He was probably going back the prescribed way, through the valleys round Avernus; or else up the plunging rocks that ringed the Devil's Throat, where the water roared. The route was possibly new to him, his steps uncertain. Monteverdi's Orpheus, who had set out carolling in triumph, now let minor chords and doubting pauses steal into his song. He was losing faith. He did not know that Eurydice was still following, and no one could assure him that she was. Perhaps he was being tricked, and a backward glance would not matter after all. Love was stronger, surely, than any rules:

> Why be afraid, my heart?
> What Pluto forbids, Love commands.

Gluck's Eurydice continued to question, weep and scold. Why couldn't he embrace her? Speak to her? At least look round? *Ma vieni e taci!* 'Just come on, and keep quiet!' was all he could answer her.

Ahead of them, suddenly, a crack of sun broke through. In the Devil's Throat they were just past the worst of the rocks, where the track twisted round for the last ascent and the spray from the waterfalls caught the bright glitter of the distant, outside air. He had never longed so much for light; yet this light was worse than the dark, for if he turned round now, nothing would obscure her. With every step the widening day stared more boldly at the face he must not see and must not imagine. At every moment his frustration grew. In Monteverdi an unnerving chord clashed behind him, as if she fell, or as if the Furies suddenly gripped her by the arm. Anouilh's Eurydice, her head pressed against Orpheus's back, saw his hesitation and cried, 'Don't look at me! Let me live!' But at the very border of light and darkness – 'just a step into the light', 'at the limit of night' – love, or self-confidence, over-came him. He turned to look at her.

Cocteau's Orpheus did not even move his head. He glanced in the rear-view mirror of the Princess's car as Eurydice, from the back seat, desperately caressed his cheek. That was enough.

And three times the thunder crashed out over Avernus.

*

It was bound to happen. Taboos existed only to be broken. Every prohibition of myth or fairytale begged to be infringed. The door that was never to be opened, small, harmless, choked with ivy, was unlocked, and let in Death. The midnight curfew was ignored, and its first banging chimes blew the satin gown to rags. The fairy purse was rubbed not three times, but four, and the gold coins turned to dust. The fruit of the Forbidden Tree was eaten, and the gates of Paradise slammed shut. On each occasion the hero was almost there, his fortune made, her happiness assured, when every dream crumbled away.

Only Monteverdi's Orpheus had consciously overreached himself, vaunting the power of love against death. In almost every other version his glance was a mistake. Nonetheless, he broke the law. The taboo was reinforced, in pictures of the scene, by Eurydice's half-naked body, the grave-clothes ravelling away from the limbs he still desired but could not have. Orpheus gazed on the form of the goddess as Acteon had stared at Artemis, her thighs in a forest pool like pure-white saplings touched with a glisten of water, a fuzz of dark moss. His gaze, as Freudians saw it, was tantamount to sexual penetration. Violent as a rape, it destroyed what he looked on.

But perhaps there was something here that he had to rebuff, because he was not ready to accept it. The feminine, intuitive, passionate side of him, possibly, that sleeping or wandering *anima* of whom he was now disturbingly aware. Or it might be, as Rilke was to write the next year, his own Death, the other side of life: unilluminated, like the other side of the moon, but essential to his completion. Orpheus had journeyed towards it and had stretched out a hand to grasp it, the intimate friend carried deep in his own darkness ('the Death that we carry inside ourselves from our birth', as Cocteau expressed it). Eurydice had held open for him the grave-door between the worlds. But he could not go further. For whatever reason, that 'great Yes . . . before eternity' could not yet be said.

He had, at least, looked at life for a brief while from Death's side. Rilke, too, had done this. At the castle of Duino near Trieste in 1911 or 1912, walking up and down in the gardens that sloped steeply to the sea, he had paused to lean on the forking branches of a tree. There, 'so pleasantly supported', he had fallen into contemplation. The most delicate vibrations began to pass through him, as though his body 'was being treated in some sort like a soul'; and he concluded that he had passed to the other side of Nature. Like a ghost, he felt he already lived elsewhere, and was looking at familiar things with a distant affection; he stood in the body as in 'a quitted window', gazing at a scene to which he had returned:

> He was looking back at things, as it were over his shoulder, and a daring, sweet flavour was added to their existence, now finished for him, as if everything had been spiced with a touch of the blossom of farewell.

But then a wind blew, his position became uncomfortable, and he stepped forward, back into life.

Eurydice in this scene was also the fleeting subconscious, brimming with obscure ambitions and desires. She was the idea not remembered, the remark unsaid, the poem unwritten; all that might have been ordered and drawn into the light, but in the end could not be. She was the past that, despite every longing, could not be recaptured. Or the dream so vivid that the dreamer, caught in a childhood street in the snow, is convinced that the melting flakes will be on his coat in the morning; but with the thought alone, the weight and pressure of it, snow and dream have vanished like a bubble.

Blind Milton, too, had such a dream. He saw his dead wife, risen from childbed, 'veiled all in white', with her face too veiled, though nothing could obscure its sweetness:

> But O as to embrace me she enclin'd
> I wak'd, she fled, and day brought back my night.

The search for mystic enlightenment also ended here. The initiate or the natural philosopher, allowed the precious burden of esoteric knowledge, would lose it immediately unless he trod the rigorous, uphill, unturning path. Doubts, temptations, demons, all attacked him. But his only care had to be his own great awakening, the union with the Beloved or with Wisdom in the light. If he turned, he would have to make the journey over again. There could be no exceptions.

Sixteenth-century painters expressed a theory close to this. Orpheus was the artist trying to grasp beauty, to snare it with a word or catch it with a brush, and failing. With this in mind Giorgione painted himself as Orpheus around 1500, exhausted, bearded, haunted, with his cloak thrown around him and Dionysian ivy wilting on his brow. The painting was rough and dark, almost smudged. He held a *lira da braccio*, upright and unplayed. In the distant background he showed himself losing Eurydice, looking back as a demon dragged her away to the fire. Now he gazed at the viewer as though he could no longer live. He was the artist emptied out completely. The beauty he loved had vanished; all was lost.

But, as Virgil reminded him, Orpheus had brought this on himself. Virgil had observed it all: the light, false confidence as he walked uphill ('he had escaped every mischance'), the sudden lack of caution, and then *furor*, *dementia*, the mad act of turning round. He believed he was safe, that she was his. You could understand it; you could even pardon it, 'if the shades of Death ever pardon'. But it was madness all the same. Orpheus thought he could trump the laws of Nature and the gods, but no man could. Though his song might be a *pharmakon*, a drug that lulled and lured the forces of Nature, his human passion made the magic worthless. In the end, he had wanted her too much.

To some, however – twentieth-century observers, by the couch or at the desk – his turn had been no accident. It was more deliberate than that, part of the conscious growth of the artist and the making of art: as when a child, told not to look at a dead bird, says, No, I will look at it, because I want to see it for myself; I want to know for myself what it is. Or when a poet, allowed a moment of intense vision, swims wildly through the murk of his own mind towards it, heedless, free, determined, though dispersing it with every stroke.

That backward glance, wrote Maurice Blanchot,

> was absolutely necessary. To look at Eurydice, without regard to the song, in the impatience and imprudence of desire which forgets the law; that *is* inspiration.

Like all artists, Orpheus could not seize her; she vanished as he looked. That moment of overwhelming desire led him directly to the source of his art, even if at once she disappeared. That was the risk he had accepted: to fail in the attempt. She had 'escaped being'; but she had also escaped 'the power of violence that forces and seizes', as the poet tried to press his inspiration into words. Once again, Mystery refused to be named or possessed.

So she had gone. But Orpheus, in Blanchot's imaginings, found himself looking at 'a point, not a point, but a bloss-oming, a smile of the whole of the space . . . a smile that was free, without hindrance, without a face, that radiated softly out from this absence, illuminated it, gave it a semblance, a name, a silent name.'

This, Blanchot wrote, was the 'extreme moment of freedom' for both of them. Orpheus, by looking, in that 'impatience of desire', had exercised the liberty he was born for. But by renouncing the power of possessing Eurydice, the inaccessible other, he had also left her free to remain as she was.

For Jung, too, the turn was deliberate. Now that Orpheus had made his shaman's journey to the Underworld, he was ready to look at life from Death's side. He had understood what he must do and what he must be. Quite consciously, he chose to turn round, because with that one glance he shattered his former identity and shocked his soul awake. This was the moment of individuation, when Orpheus acknowledged the particular Fate that awaited him: to be killed, to be scattered, to enter the state of being that Eurydice had already discovered. He did not embrace Death, as she had. He could not do that yet. But he looked Death in the face and, at the same time, he released Eurydice to remain there. As he had claimed her in love, so in love he let her go. In Rilke's words:

> Is it not time that, in loving,
> we freed ourselves from the loved one, and, shivering,
> endured: as the arrow endures the string,
> to become, in the gathering out-leap, something more than
> itself?
> For staying is nowhere.

When Orpheus looked back, he also assured his survival as a poet. He became who he was meant to be. As Mallarmé put it, he was 'changed into himself'. All men and women who longed to excel, Jung thought, should have the courage to turn round as he had done.

Yet he threw everything away, insisted Boethius's stern, far, sixth-century voice. Orpheus, the human soul, having plumbed the depths of life and death, having fled the body and the earth, had almost gained enlightenment. The spiritual discipline of his ordeal in Hell was about to make him immortal. Divine splendour glimmered just ahead. But then he looked back at material things, at the dark, and was confounded. At the very point of union with God, the glorious end of human longing, he was floored by human desire; and lost what he loved. *Vidit, perdidit, occidit.*

> Whoever seeks the upward way,
> Lift your mind into the day;
> For who gives in and turns his eye
> Back to the darkness from the sky,
> Loses while he looks below
> All that up with him may go.

'No man,' added Jesus in Luke's gospel, 'having put his hand to the plough, and looking back, is fit for the kingdom of God.'

But 'Who to love can give a law?' Boethius sighed. 'Love unto itself is law.'

*

A three-figure bas-relief, carved in Athens around 400 BC and known in several Roman copies, seemed to show the moment of looking back as one of tender regret. Eurydice's left hand was on Orpheus's shoulder, just below his fox-skin cap, as if she leaned on him to let him guide her; one foot was still in the act of walking forward. Hermes stood discreetly beside them, Eurydice's right hand firmly clasped in his. Orpheus's hand touched hers and, almost incidentally, brushed her veil aside. Each gazed upon the other with the steady impassiveness of love. Both Orpheus and his lyre were reduced to silence.

Rilke, seeing this bas-relief in Rome, assumed it was the

moment of parting: of Eurydice re-released into the new life she had embraced. Orpheus was in shock, Hermes agonised; but she felt nothing. Though she still touched his shoulder – a gesture Rilke found expressive of the deepest feeling – it was without possessiveness or sadness. They were simply 'two images', distant from each other, that had 'gently come together in the unprovable inner depths of a mirror':

> And when, abruptly,
> the god had halted her and, with an anguished
> outcry spoke the words: He has turned round! –
> she took in nothing, and said softly: *Who?*

This was the end. Hermes was now in charge again. She turned to go, still hampered by her grave-clothes: 'uncertain, gentle, and without impatience', as she had always been.

Virgil did not record any quiet leave-taking. There was no time. Orpheus saw her, and for an instant moved to hug her, but she had already dissipated like smoke into the air:

> *ceu fumus in auras*
> *commixtus tenuis, fugit diversa . . .*

Her fading arms jerked towards him, but the dark pulled her roughly down into itself. Virgil heard her scream: 'Orpheus, we are ruined, you and I! What dreadful madness is this? See how the cruel Fates are calling me back again, and my swimming eyes are drowned in darkness! Goodbye for ever. I'm swept away, wrapped in endless night, and the powerless hands I stretch towards you are yours no longer!'

> *invalidasque tibi tendens, heu! non tua, palmas.*

The wedded, interwoven souls were unravelling, *me* from *you*, *yours* from *mine*. And the winds he had never felt here, to which he had sung on the shore when she had first died, now carried her away with them.

Ovid, his grief less sharp, observed a quieter scene. Eurydice had died a second time, he wrote. But she did not reproach her husband, 'for what could he be blamed for, except for love?' With the faintest of farewells, one soft *vale*, she fell back through the shadows of the lower world.

Orpheus rushed after her, plunging down through the rocks to rescue her again. But the almost-girl had faded away into infinite jumbled darkness, like Chaos before creation. Half-running, half-falling, his hands at any moment ready to clutch on nothing, Orpheus careered to the edge of the Styx. He begged Charon to ferry him across a second time. The grizzled boatman pushed him aside, and laughed.

Eurydice, meanwhile, passed out of history. Virgil saw her already wrapped and shrouded, floating on the Stygian barge. In painting after painting the fogs of Hades over-whelmed the slim, pale girl who still stared towards the light, and the man in the light. Her tears remained as white crystalline streaks on the slopes of the eastern Rhodopes. (Orpheus's own tears grew there as blue campanula, springing from the rock that once more appeared to contain her sleeping form.) And in the underpass at Waterloo Station in London her sad thoughts on that journey back, as the poet Sue Hubbard heard them, were engraved in 2003 on the concrete tunnel walls. Her melancholy echoed in the whistle of distant trains.

Will you forget me? Steel tracks lead you out
past cranes and crematoria,
boat yards and bike sheds, ruby shards
of roman glass and wolf-bone mummified in mud,
the rows of curtained windows like eyelids
heavy with sleep, to the city's green edge.

Now I stop my ears with wax, hold fast
The memory of the song you once whispered in my ear,
Its echoes tangle like briars in my thick hair.

You turned to look.

Socrates thought Orpheus had been bound to fail. For all his
high thoughts, he was a weakling, 'a mere harpist', the Argonaut
without armour who sat out the most dangerous under-
takings. Such a man would never die for the highest love, as
philosophy required. Instead he had slipped alive into the
Underworld, and what Hades had granted him was the mere
phantom (*phasma*) of his wife. So much for poets, who dealt
only in illusions and copies of what was real.

Imagine anyway going to get your *wife*, sneered Martial.
No wonder all Hell was amazed at it. If Pluto wanted to punish
Orpheus for trespassing, of course he would give her back to
him! And if he wanted to thank him for his playing, what
greater boon than to take her away again!

Plutarch claimed that Orpheus had managed only half the
journey anyway. He had stopped at a place where dreams were
made, for the Underworld was their source. Dazzling white

water and brightly coloured streams (unity and plurality in their philosophical meanings) were poured into a basin in the foggy air, where spirits mixed them together. The white water symbolised truth in dreams, the colours deceptions. Orpheus assumed that the basin was an oracle, shared equally by bright Apollo and Night, his Mother of Dreams. He was wrong about that, in Plutarch's opinion. But he stopped and watched, increasingly fascinated by the work of the spirits in the rainbow mist; he took mental notes to be written up later in his book *Krater*, or *The Mixing Bowl*; and he forgot to bring Eurydice back from the dead.

Others thought the journey had in fact gone well. A shaman who crossed into the land of Death could not fail in his mission, any more than the Earth could cease to give back life or the sun could fail to rise. So Orpheus led Eurydice without in-cident up to the light. The earliest versions of the journey, before Virgil established the unhappy ending, contained no conditions or looking back. Funerary vases and *stelae* of antiq-uity were painted or carved in the belief that he had saved her, and could therefore save others. On Roman tombstones they confidently held hands. The famous Attic bas-relief could be interpreted as the joyous reunion of lower self and soul, their faces full of calm wonder rather than blank regret. Or Eurydice was perhaps the revelation granted to Orpheus by Persephone: her own shadow, or Wisdom, gently touching him and allowing him, at last, to lift the veil and gaze on her. Orpheus himself, in 'his' book *The Veil*, apparently understood this moment as the transition to immortality, the final removal of the coverings of Death.

The secrets she had told him only Cocteau's Orpheus heard.

They kissed before she spoke: a long, exploratory kiss, pent-up over the years. The Power she obeyed, said the Princess, lived 'nowhere'. 'Some believe he thinks about us; others that he thinks us up. Others, that he sleeps and that we are his dream – his bad dream.' As for how his orders reached her, they were 'passed on and on, like the tam-tams of Africa, or mountain echoes, or the leaves of the forest'. Orpheus had already heard that song.

Several medieval versions, too, contrived some sort of happy outcome. Orpheus and Eurydice emerged lightly from the dragon-jaws of Hell, leaving behind blue devils. They were chatting and laughing about love-games; he in his floppy velvet *bonnet*, playing his lute, she dainty in pointed shoes. Together they processed up a winding road to the palace of Marriage and Love. Sir Orfeo, with swift strides, got Queen Heurodis out and returned to Traciens, where eventually he revealed his true identity and ruled his people again.

Indeed, when he represented Love, Orpheus was often supposed to triumph over Death. Composers' patrons required it. When his story was chosen for telling in music, always favourite and first, the resolution had to be in a major key. In the earliest opera, written by Jacopo Peri for the wedding of Henri IV and Maria de' Medici in 1600, Orpheus embraced Eurydice unreservedly in the final scene. This was perhaps too bold, the librettist admitted, 'but it seemed fitting'. Monteverdi in 1607 contrived a flying machine from which Apollo descended, putting an end to Orpheus's self-indulgent and unrelenting grief. He would see Eurydice again, the god assured him: her 'beautiful semblance' would shine in the sun and the stars, and Orpheus himself would be immortal, along with her. But a rebuke was also in order from heavenly father to son, who had learned nothing from his sojourn in the world:

> *Ancor non sai*
> *Come nulla quà giù diletta e dura?*

> Do you still not know that nothing here below
> Delights and lasts?

In Gluck's opera too, though robed, restrained and sober, Orpheus could not be allowed a tragic ending. It had to be changed, as Gluck admitted 'to accommodate the legend to our theatre'. So at first his Orpheus despaired, shaking Eurydice's dead body, weeping, and singing out of his weeping one of the loveliest arias in opera, for he could not conceive what he would do or where he would go without her:

> *Che farò senz' Eurydice,*
> *Dove andrò senza il mio ben?*
> *Che farò, dove andrò?*

But then Love appeared to him, white-wigged and silver-quivered, declaring 'You have suffered enough.' Eurydice had not died, merely fainted away; she could be revived; and the couple, transfigured with joy, strolled together to the Temple where Love dwelled. A ballet sealed their happiness.

Many in the first-night audience objected to this ending, as they also complained about the weird orange backcloths through which Orpheus wandered in the Elysian Fields (authentic ancient colours, Gluck maintained, the tints of autumn and dead souls). But an anonymous reviewer, writing in the *Wienerisches Diarium* of October 13th 1762, was not at all offended. Herr Calzabigi, the librettist, had certainly changed the story, but 'how reasonably!' His Orpheus was neither foolish nor despicable, just a good man led astray by love, and 'a lapse caused by love can be rectified by none better than the god of love'. Besides,

> the audience, who would otherwise have gone home saddened by shared suffering, are most grateful to [Herr Calzabigi] for this happy alteration. And anyway, since Orpheus is so virtuous throughout, hasn't he deserved a happier fate?

Czeslaw Milosz thought so. He took the road from Hell with him in 2004, shortly after the death of his own wife. When Orpheus turned round, he found no one behind him. But the sun, sky and clouds of the world he came back to were full of Eurydice. She was scattered and given away, like rain, and he fell asleep on earth that was scented and warmed by her.

In Ovid, as in Virgil, the scene was far different. Orpheus had learned nothing in the land of the dead. He sat for seven days on the bank of the Styx, weeping. His beard grew, and the filthy river water soiled his clothes. In the Devil's Throat cave he did not stir from the twist in the track by the waterfall, where he had turned round. His effigy is still there, near a constant trickle of water out of the rock that is known as 'Orpheus's tears'. If you leave a ten-*stotinki* coin there and wash your face with the water, your sins will be forgiven. But his were not. Brutally, he had been cast back to dwell on his failure alone. One twelfth-century text declared that he eventually built a second tomb for Eurydice, covered with laurels, gems and gold, with these words inscribed above the entrance: 'Killed by her husband at the gates of Hell.'

In his sorrow he returned to the Thracian plains, where for one brief spell they had been happy. Remembrance was only keener there. Desperate, he wandered for three years through the Rhodopes, across the Hyperborean ice and as far as the Arctic snow. Virgil, in a tender touch, saw him trudging through 'fields that were never widowed of the Riphaean frosts'. The grass was sharp with sorrow, the trees glassy with it, the hills cracked over with relentless pain. He cried 'Eurydice!' as though she could be found there, among the ice-edged leaves and stones. As he walked, the snow clogging and hardening his fawn-skin boots, he brought the winter with his grief. The wind battered and tore him and, though he might have calmed it, he no longer tried.

After Eurydice's first death he had sung away his heartache. With her second death, Music itself had died. As his last notes faded into the blackening sky, light, life and order vanished from the world.

At last he settled in a cave under Pangaion where the River Strymon flowed into the sea, and entered the realm of silence.

Sandman: The Song of Orpheus, 1991

Sixth string: Fame

Months passed. One painter saw him lying on the sand, half-rolled in his blue cloak, inert, with his lyre clutched to him. No one came that way. From the sea-marsh the cranes rose up and headed south, birds of fortune and awakening song, flying too high for him to notice them.

Propped now against a rock, his eyes dull, he gazed out across marsh and sea: the sea of generation, the shifting sublunary world.

Water, he had sung,

> is death for soul, and earth is death
> for water.

Opposites resisted or absorbed each other, and that constant motion kept the world alive. *It is not lawful to stand still.* Yet soul wearied and sickened in that atmosphere, as in the damp, tuneless strings of his unplayed lyre.

He had also taught that the body was the soul's sepulchre. *Soma, sema,* body, tomb: words that were almost identical, and heavy as earth. He had been the first to make a play on them; Plato later copied him. Original sin, the Titans' crime against the child Dionysus, had made this imprisonment necessary –

necessary even for him, a god's son. So his soul had fallen into the sea, the water muffling and crushing him down to the black depths; he had soaked into the sand, like the last gleaming traces of the retreating tide. And then the body had encased him. Drowned and buried, deep in noxious marsh-mud like the uninitiated souls he had seen in Cocytus, he waited for the cycle to reverse itself:

> but water escapes from earth,
> and from water comes soul again
> burning, transforming Aether –

The sun rose over the Aegean before him and set behind him. The wheel of life cast its ever-moving light on the sea and the blank, reflecting sky. He observed it without caring. His songs beside Strymon, Seneca said, had a single theme: all that is born must die. For months he could not raise himself even to those words.

Potentially the sea could comfort him. He had sung of it as the enfolding guardian and boundary of all things, the earthly form of all-moving Ocean and blue-cloaked, blue-eyed Tethys, mother of the clouds, flowing with streams and rivers from which the gods were born. During his voyage to Colchis Tethys had placed her hand on the rudder-blade of the *Argo* to guide it through the booming, wandering rocks, and her attendant nymphs had lifted their slim white arms above the water, singing, to pass the ship like a ball between them. On summer days the colours of her cloak, from pale turquoise to purple, were woven in layers through the deeply spreading water, and her playfulness was in the loop and dip of her waves towards the shore. There, too, their foam sparkled and gathered, like the glittering seed or sperm of Heaven from which Aphrodite rose, all-connecting, bright-haired, the grace-giver, laughing and proclaiming Love:

> Come in your swan-drawn chariot over the waves,
> joy in the creatures of the deep fast-circling, swimming,
> or with the sea-tanned nymphs dance over land,
> light on the yellow sands, embracing, skimming . . .

He could not recover that love-lightness now. Aphrodite's laughter seemed as hollow as the boom of the collapsing and disordered waves. If the goddess had been born there, there was birth-blood in the water and afterbirth, gelatinous as dark seaweed, washed up on the shore. It was still true that Love controlled everything. But 'dreadful Necessity', or Fate, was stronger.

Slowly he detached himself from all he saw and heard, retreating into the dry, calcified shell. This was another sort of death. He lay on the shore, face-down in the gritty sand, emptied utterly. Picked up in a curious hand, he would weigh nothing, could give nothing, would sing nothing into the ear, but would be cast away to clink across the rocks and be rolled in the spume, worthless. At night the stars no longer shone on him, but sea and sky in a black undifferentiated wall blocked everything that might be light, or opening, or hope.

Monteverdi gave him Echo as a companion, the far, faint double of his grieving. But Echo, like a mirror, threw back the truth of his sad self-delusions. 'I haven't mourned her enough,' he whispered; Echo sighed, 'Enough.'

Non hò pianto però tanto che basti.
Echo: *Basti.*

Winter flung violence over this scene. Blue-maned Poseidon, deep-roaring, earth-shaking, crashed in his chariot out of the sea. Storms and purifying winds, Thracian Boreas and the rest of them, thrashed the shoreline and tore the leaves from the trees. They whipped white horses out of the surf, manes streaming with spray, and drove the gulls tumbling like foam-wisps along them until the gale was spent. The sun rose then over the sour, smoking shield of the sea, copper-red and dinted with rain.

From the cave Orpheus watched, pulling his thin cloak round him, pressing his back against rock that was now impervious and immovable, in silence.

Yet Rilke, filled with Orpheus's own song-breath, could offer comfort. In silence all music began, as well as ended. From desolation came transformation:

Be always ahead of farewell like a thing that's behind you,
speeding away like a winter about to depart.
For among winters one infinite winter will find you,
Which, overwintered, will prove the resolve of your heart.

Be ever dead in Eurydice, – rise up more singingly,
rise and regain that pure kinship to which you belong.
Here, in the realm of the vanishing, sing out more ringingly;
Be! like a glass that shatters itself in its song.

*

Under the Strymon cliff, under the stars, Virgil came upon him alone. The night was cold, and he was weeping. Music crept from him, but barely. His songs were no longer those praising cosmogonies of gods and creation, but of himself, and of pain. Without soundness of body, he wrote once, 'everything is useless'. Perhaps he spoke with feeling. His hymns often asked for health, 'gentle-handed', like a woman's caress.

Shadowy forms stole round him: rustling oaks with the stars in their branches, soft-footed tigers with eyes like the ember-sparks of a fire. He sang as the nightingale did in the shade of the poplar, mourning the young she had lost:

> Weeping all night, on a branch repeating the piteous song,
> Loading the acres round with the burden of her lament.

Henryson heard the words of the song. It began with a simple question: *What art thou, love?*

> Quhat art thou lufe how sall i the dyffyne
> Bitter and suete cruel and merciable
> Plesand to sum til othir playnt and pyne
> To sum constant till other variabil
> Hard is thy law thi bandis unbreakable . . .

Many months later, Ovid found him. Time seemed to have begun to heal. He was singing lightly, as beautifully as ever, of love, death and change. Yet what was loved was often lost, accidentally and randomly, by the throw of a discus, the thrust of a boar's tusk, the grazing flight of an arrow. And Calliope ('O Muse, my mother!') was once again the woman to whom he sang.

Especially now he told stories of young men and women

turned into trees. Their skin hardened; a rind grew on them, imprisoning calves, thighs, elbows, as they struggled desperately to escape, merely to move. Branches broke from their shoulders, out of the white flesh. Blood thickened into sap, muscle to unbending wood; their hair coarsened and thinned into leaves, while their rooting toenails hooked down grimly into the earth. He had watched the Hesperides grow into trees gracefully, laughingly, like beckoning dancers; Eurydice he had stroked loose with love from the crushing, aching wood. Now bitter Fate, time after time, battened and bludgeoned his lovers into place.

The sun was high, the day hot, and Orpheus sang without shade on the thin turf of a mountaintop. But the trees moved to him:

> Jupiter's great oak, with its lofty branches, soft lime trees and beeches, and the virgin laurel; brittle hazels, and ash trees that are used for spear-shafts, smooth firs and the holm oak, bowed down with acorns; the genial sycamore; the variegated maple, willows that grow by the rivers, and the water-loving lotus; evergreen box, slender tamarisks, double-hued myrtles, viburnum with its dark blue berries. Ivy too, trailing its tendrils, and leafy vines, vine-clad elms and mountain ash, pitchpine and wild strawberry . . .

Each brought its own shadow. He was cooled by the feather-shade of tamarisks, scented flickerings of limes, ash like a cloak of interlocking fingers, sycamore in splashes of dark and light. Together they made a *nemus*, or sacred grove, protecting him and bending to his songs. And among them – as Orpheus perhaps acknowledged with a dip of the head, having sung their stories – Phaeton's shivering sisters stood as white, amber-dropping poplars, the priest Attis as a quiet, straight pine, and beautiful weeping Cyparissus as a cypress, slim and dense-green in grief. In the grove, as much as in the Underworld, he was surrounded by ghosts of his own making.

Would-be disciples continued to seek him out in his wanderings. His ideas were extraordinary, especially the notion that man was half-divine and might have eternal life. He had been to Hades, had discerned its secrets and could placate the gods who ruled there. In his recent loneliness he had come so close to all the gods, Ficino thought, that he had learned to think as they did. He knew the rituals of purity and the ways of deliverance from the 'sorrowful, weary circle' of existence in the world.

His *Argonautica* contained a sort of prospectus of what he offered. Besides his books, and the rites he had established,

> you have learned the ways of divination,
> by beasts and birds, and what the order of entrails,
> and what is presaged in their dream-roaming paths
> by souls of mortals overcome in sleep;
> answers to signs and portents, the stars' courses . . .
> > And I have told you all I saw and learned
> > when I to Taenarus walked the dark road of Hades
> > trusting my cithara, for love of my wife . . .

In particular he was known as a revealer of mysteries: not merely secrets, but *mystikon*, unutterable things, such as the real names of the gods. Pythagoras learned his teachings as part of his own initiation in the Thracian Mysteries, and took him as his prophet, as well as his model of the pure, perfected life. Such a life, Orpheus wrote, unstained by sin or pleasure, was the key to recognising 'divine signs' in oracles and dreams.

Every evening, as darkness fell over mountain and forest, he conducted ceremonies of purification, incense and fire. All things began here, in the dark. Night was the time when the visible faded and the mind was laid open to mystery. After the busily heating and generating sun, Night nourished and cooled, like a nurse, as he addressed her; never rising, never setting, simply coming into quiet dominion when the sun departed. From the 'innermost shrine' of her cave within the cosmos, or in man, Night spoke. The land returned then to no forms or colours, and waited to recover them out of the dark as Orpheus had tried.

This, the time of the slow-stalking fox and the nightingale's saddest songs, was also his moment for instruction and initiation, 'sealing while illuminating'. His hymns were composed to be sung then. They accompanied the lighting of torches and the burning of myrrh, storax, manna and frankincense, the perfumed essence of the trees he sang to life. Each incense was appropriate to the god addressed, diffusing their influence into the breath, and hence the souls, of those who worshipped. In ecstasy, the worshippers too might burn up into the nature of the god.

Amid the thick, white, rolling plumes, prayers were offered by the *mystai*, or initiates, to the moon (with storax), Apollo (pounded frankincense), Aether (saffron), the water nymphs (aromatics), Ocean, Zeus, the Furies, the dawn, the winds, the divinity of dreams. Orpheus, by invoking these gods and elements, made visions of them appear: Ocean flooding and crashing in boiling spume and shingle, Artemis pouring down her arrows on the sleeping, silvered trees, Aether arching silently in glitter-light from pole to pole. Come, he sang, come. Night was invoked with flaming brands, which emphasised her beauty.

Diodorus remembered hearing such hymns sung; they were 'exceptionally melodious'. Pausanias said they were few and short, and not as beautiful as Homer's. But they were considered holier. Diodorus called their dialect 'archaic' – meaning, some supposed, that it was closer to the language of the gods who had given Orpheus instruction. Plato thought there could be nothing sweeter, though he did not grace them with the name of poetry; they were prophecies, or instructions. The hymns that survive from several centuries later sound, more than anything, like conjuror's incantations. When Proclus was ill, his friends sang the hymns together to soothe him and cheer themselves. And Pico della Mirandola, writing in the fifteenth century, thought there was nothing more effective in natural magic than these strange, epithet-laden, repetitive prayers – if sung to the proper music, and with proper concentration.

Pico, like Ficino (his teacher and rival, whom he mercilessly criticised), was not prepared to say more in public. But he had derived his own magic from Orpheus's hymns, and knew that the gods invoked there were not 'deceiving demons', but 'divine virtues'. The hymns might be suitable, therefore, for Christian ears, despite Ficino's doubts. Symbolically and secretly, they were about divine creative power, in which man also shared. In parts, Pico wrote, they were like the Kabbalah, in which he was expert. Not evil, but good. Not dark, but light.

Orpheus, as the high priest of the rite, sponsored the initiands and led them, as he had tried to lead Eurydice, through the night to the dawn. 'The Rape of Persephone' was re-enacted, as well as 'The Descent to Hades': he had composed them specifically for this. Re-enactments and sacrifices were both ways to *katharsis*, or purification of the soul. Blessed Memory, 'sweet and vigilant', was invoked to remind the initiands what they had been and where they had come from. The candidates, both men and women, were also sprinkled with holy water, or handed an egg – creation in miniature, incubating Life – into which their impurities were transferred. The sacrament they consumed was no longer bloody flesh, but cakes dipped in pinkish, resinous pine-honey at 'the sacred ritual of the table'. At dawn they drank goat's milk into which more honey had been stirred, the first sweet food of Orpheus's birth-chamber and the nectar of immortal souls.

No initiate ever revealed these things. They had sworn not to, 'by Fire and Water, Earth and Sky, Sun and Moon, Phanes and Night', oaths that kept their force for centuries. But Clement of Alexandria provided more breathless details of the mysteries he credited to Orpheus. 'This is what they say,' he wrote. '*I have fasted, I have drunk the cup; I have received from the box; having done, I put it into the basket, and out of the basket into the chest.*' But what was 'it', exactly? And what was in those mystic chests? A cross between conjuror's props and schoolboy's tuck:

sesame cakes, and pyramidal cakes, and globular and flat cakes, embossed all over, and lumps of salt, and a serpent, the symbol of Dionysus Bassareus . . . And pomegranates, and branches, and rods, and ivy leaves . . . and round cakes and poppy seeds . . . and marjoram, and a lamp, and a sword . . .

Orpheus's golden sword, perhaps, curved like a Thracian scimitar. And as for the cakes, the Derveni Papyrus suggested he sacrificed these to the crowds of 'impeding demons' who came in search of souls, tossing them out like crusts to dogs.

Clement also found squills there, the small dried bulbs of dark-blue flowers. Bulbs in general, boiled and eaten, were thought to enhance sexual prowess. In Orpheus's case he may have laid them on the altar to keep evil spells away. His other holy objects were also placed there: the apples of rebirth, the ball of the Earth as he had seen it from afar, the polished mirror where Death appeared. The chests themselves represented the holy casket that Apollo had used to hold the heart of Dionysus. It was all that survived of him after his scattering, the receptacle of his soul.

Dionysus remained Orpheus's god. Eight of his hymns paid homage to the 'mad, furious inspirer', and the wine god's symbols were reverently carried in procession. He was still worshipped – with almost all forms of incense, 'and a libation of milk, too' – as the boy-god of spring, 'who puts to sleep and wakes up the years', appearing as a dancer with the glow of joy on his face. But his revels now brought calm. 'Slaughter' was still mentioned, though it now meant the death-like stripping away of material things; the torn god's 'limbs' were still gathered, but as an act of Apollonian order and remembrance. ('Take up all the parts of Wine [Dionysus] in the cosmos,' ran one precept, 'and bring them to me.') New regulations showed how deeply the ceremonies had changed. 'Within the place of sacrifice,' they ran, 'no one is to make a noise, or clap his hands, or sing, but each man is to say his part and do it in all quietness and order as the priest and the *Archibacchos* direct.' If anyone noisily infringed the rule, the thyrsus of the god was set up against him (the bobbing, leafing phallus now a sober staff) and he was required to leave. 'Breathe on me,' one of the Dionysus hymns ended, 'in a spirit of perfect kindness.'

The initiand wore white linen now, with a hood of white linen pulled over his head. White clay was dusted on his face to make him a being of the other world. But initiation was no gentler than it had been before. Orpheus yelled riddles at him, thrust mirrors in his face, whirled the bull-roarer until it howled like the Thracian wind. Veiled and tightly blindfolded, the candidate was led by a priestess stumbling through rocks and across high unrailed bridges, while other *mystai* with white-smeared faces screamed and writhed around him. One witness reported fearful, disorienting sounds as the dancers leapt, with flashing alternations of light and dark. Fires blazed up, and were doused. The whirling drums banged out once more, beat after beat. An initiate remembered 'wanderings and tiresome windings, gruesome and futile journeyings through the darkness; then, before the end, all those powerful sensations, shivering and trembling, sweating and horror'. In sheer terror, gripping the hand of the priestess so desperately that he almost broke it, he enacted his own death. Then it ended, the blindfold was pulled back, he saw light. Beautiful, mystical, blazing – his.

The weary initiand, still bucking with fear, was helped into the ritual circle. He collapsed on a sacred throne to hear Orpheus's teachings read. More lost poems, 'The Girdling' and 'The Ritual Robing', suggested that he was costumed as the sun, Ocean and the stars. A garland of poplar leaves, the tree of the Spring of Memory, was hung around his neck. He took a trembling communion: a crumble of sweet barley-cakes on his tongue, a draught of chalk-white goat's milk from a clay beaker, with the white gypsum still tight on his cheeks. Exhausted, he pressed his face to the breasts of the priestess who played Persephone. She told him he was blessed, happy, a god. He was pure now. 'Vile impulses' and 'loathesome thoughts' had been cleansed from his mind. His soul had been passed through the winnowing sieve, blown new by brutal, then tender, gusts of wind. 'To die in life is to become life,' Rumi wrote, many centuries later:

the wind stops skirting you, and enters.

Initiation, the return to the beginning, 'wakened the memory of sublime things'.

The worshippers now danced in sober, slower measures around the clearing. Orpheus, or an initiand, made the fixed centre, the soul in the body or the sun in the cosmos; the dancers made the ceaseless weaving of existence, the seasons, the soul-carrying winds, the vortices of fish and birds swarming to the lyre, the returning hours. In particular, at Orpheus's direction, they made the seven movements of the planets circling the sun: around, forwards, backwards, up, down, to the right, to the left, while the initiand watched them, calmer now, sinking into trance. As always, men and stars were linked together. In dance the blessed gods became apparent, unwearying, all-moving, all-connecting, whirling overhead in great fire-wheels of creative force that turned, too, in the singing forms below them. At the height of the dancing the gods were called; and they came down blazing, life overflowing, filling minds and hearts.

Afterwards, exhausted, the *mystai* slept in their white robes. Sleep was invoked with the burning of a single poppy on the altar. Orpheus played, again, the deepest string, and intoned a chant without sounding the words. Near-silence allowed long-winged dreams, 'soft-stealing, whispering to the mind', to open the intellectual sight and reveal the future. Sleep brought the 'deathlike rest' that whispered to him in the western breezes. On a stone in the clearing four red petals, licked with momentary flame, subsided to a wisp of ash.

Men and women still became the god, but not as they had done before.

The new rites were even more exclusive. 'Many are the thyrsus-bearers,' ran a tag that Plato quoted, 'but few the *Bacchoi*': few the followers who had achieved purification and union with the god. This was no mass religion, but a scattering of small, like-minded groups of the seeking or self-satisfied. Their own souls saved, they cared little for other people's. They would not consort with crowds, and their burial grounds were segregated. They avoided public baths and even the public roads; they turned aside onto footpaths, slipped into streams. Stand-offish silence was preferred to conversation. Aristophanes in the *Frogs*, around 420 BC, caught their smugness exactly:

> For us alone is there sun
> and sacred daylight,
> for we are initiated
> and righteous in our behaviour
> towards strangers
> and ordinary people.

Orpheus's most secret teachings, he told his disciples, came from 'long ago, even from Phanes', almost further than mortal intelligence could go. They contained 'the keys that open and close'. But very few could grasp them. The author of the Derveni Papyrus, while noting how carefully Orpheus had named things, confessed that his poetry was still 'strange and riddling to people'; that he used words as screens, did not mean men to understand them, and wrote so obscurely that every word needed explaining. His mentions of Phanes, too, meant nothing to most fifth-century Greeks. That deity was a foreigner, imported from Asia Minor via Thrace, and not in their mythology. Even gods they recognised became, in Orpheus's hands, strangely abstract and bloodless. When he spoke of 'silver sinews' in the air you had to guess, somehow, that the river god Achelous was hiding there. When he mentioned 'Zeus ruling on Olympus' he meant, apparently, Air ruling over Time, with Time lying 'lovely', 'white', even 'snow-capped' under the god's brooding power. Zeus, then, was Air, but most particularly he was Mind, and his wisdom in motion 'always and through everything' was *moira*, the Fate men understood as their own. This, at least, was what the Derveni author thought Orpheus meant at the most secret level; but he, too, might have read his riddles in the wrong way.

Orpheus's moral code was perplexing, also. The notion that conduct on earth might affect life after death – that the soul could be pure or impure, a moral entity rather than a mere life-breath – seemed bizarre. In the *Hippolytus* of Euripides, Theseus sneered at his son, an initiate: so he was above the common herd, was he? The chaste one, untouched by evil, the companion of the gods? 'Go on, keep boasting then, adopt a meatless diet and play the showman with your food, make Orpheus your lord and indulge in mystic rites, hold the vapourings of his books in honour! You should avoid men like that, and their holy-sounding words.' The playwright Alexis, in one comedy, imagined strongman Heracles turning down Orpheus's books in favour of one on cookery. And Antisthenes, founder of the Cynic school, had a dusty answer for the priest who initiated him into Orpheus's Mysteries with a promise of 'good things in the shades below': 'Why don't *you* die, then?'

There were many doubters. Aristophanes, again, had fun with the clay-dusting, the invocation of clouds and Orpheus's whole creation story, just right for birds:

> Chuck your schoolbooks away. This is IT.
> First of all there was nothing. No light,
> No existence. Just emptiness, space.
> In that fathomless, featureless dark,
> Night mated with Storm, laid an egg,
> And began all creation. Desire,

Golden-winged, iridescent, aglow,
Hatched and mated with Emptiness; birds
Were their nestlings, first creatures of light.
Soon the rest of the universe hatched:
Mother Earth, Sky, Sea, the gods above.
We're the oldest powers, heirs of Desire,
    And we'll prove it.

Strabo dismissed Orpheus as a village wizard, a charlatan playing for money, who later became a pedlar of prophecies and rites for initiations. A rabble followed him, he said, who puffed him up into thinking he was more than he was. Pausanias, too, said that Orpheus was proud, considering himself too good and his mysteries too important to enter the annual competition at Delphi for the best hymn sung to Apollo. He would have won it outright, of course, if he had bothered.

Plato worried that the poet's teachings were used by itinerant priests and spell-mongers, *Orpheotelestai*, who offered in his name immortality and cheap forgiveness of sins. They had 'stacks' of his books for sale, piled up in bags on the backs of mangy asses, as well as ritual instructions for sacrifices and 'childish games which they call mysteries'. Armed with these, they knocked at rich people's doors – and, surprisingly, made converts there. Some credulous buyers got themselves initiated every month, and took the children along. Clement of Alexandria, writing much later, thought there was always a streak of the sorcerer about Orpheus: spells, charms, superstitious monthly washings. In the fourth century AD Athanasius warned his readers about old women who 'for twenty *obols* or a glass of wine . . . disgorge a spell of Orpheus at you.' The spell, a piece of quackery, would have been sung, of course; a croak from toothless gums, followed by a witch's laugh.

In Virgil's *Eclogues* the shepherd Titynus, thinking of Orpheus singing, imagined the moon drawn down from Heaven and the 'cold snake' bursting in the grass. He saw gold-globed apples hanging from oaks, narcissi flowering on the alders – Orpheus's trees – and rich amber trickling from the tamarisks. Apollonian light, or spells, had transformed all of them. If he, Titynus, could sing as sweetly ('owls vying with swans', he admitted), he too could work miracles and melt his lover's heart.

This wonder-working Orpheus strolled into medieval times, and later. He could heal and do magic with his music, with herbs he had picked in the woods, with a pocketful of stones. His *Lithica*, which even Milton took seriously, recommended white crystal for kidney trouble, agate spotted 'like a lion skin' to bring good fortune, and an amulet of his favourite sea-skimming *kouralion* to ward off evil charms. Curing snake-bite was of course his speciality, as well as soothing melancholy and perking up the narcoleptic – though his music, as far as most people knew, had never saved anyone from death.

Somewhere underneath all this lay a system of philosophy. But as the Enlightenment unfolded, those few who made Orpheus their teacher (rather than a simple symbol of music, or poetry, or love) were increasingly relegated to the realm of the odd, or the mad.

*

At 9 Manor Place, Walworth, the lamp often burned late. It could be seen flickering in a window until two or three o'clock in the morning. Thomas Taylor, 'the English Pagan', wished it would burn longer. Even as a boy, feverishly teaching himself mathematics rather than suffering the lessons at St Paul's, he kept a tinder-box under his pillow for night reading. In 1785 he invented a perpetual lamp powered with oil, salt and phosphorus, but it exploded – the room being too warm – while he was demonstrating it to an audience in the Freemasons' Tavern. This, he noted sadly, 'raised a prejudice against the invention which could never afterwards be removed.'

Isaac Disraeli (father of Benjamin), in his forgotten novel *Vaurien* of 1797, once pretended to have paid Taylor a visit at home. He had to cool his heels until 'the Platonist' had finished his morning worship, a long hymn to Apollo; he then ventured upstairs. 'From the ceiling of the study', he wrote:

> depended a polished globe of silvered glass, which strongly reflected the beams of the sun. Amidst this aching splendour sat the Platonist, changing his seat with the motions of his god, so that in the course of the day he and the sun went regularly round the apartment. He was occupied in constructing a magic lanthorn . . .
>
> 'But here is the great difficulty [he explained]. How shall I represent the intolerable effulgence of the divine light? Much it grieves me, that for this sublime purpose a candle and a piece of coloured tin are all I can get into the lanthorn.'

What Taylor was working on in the 1780s, when he was in his twenties (and attempted again, with 'considerable Emendations, Alterations, and Additions', in the early 1820s), was his own translation of the eighty-seven hymns of Orpheus. Their crowded epithets and relentless hexameters resisted English poetic style, but he was putting them into rhyming couplets:

> Einodian Hecate, Trivia, lovely dame,
> Of earthly, wat'ry, and celestial frame

and, lest that seem too airy and artless, he was buttressing them with notes on their secret meaning, and on the progressions and relations of the gods. These were in tiny type that punished both eye and brain, but he had them on best Neoplatonist authority, mostly from Proclus.

A rich doctor-friend with a Harley Street practice had agreed to pay for the first edition. Few others would help him publish either that or any of his translations from Plato, Iamblichus, Proclus or Plotinus. Consquently, a very small number of copies left the press. His version of Pausanias's *Guide to Greece* was the only work that made him much money, or found general favour with the public. But, as a bookseller once remarked, 'Nothing will break the heart of Mr Taylor.' He laboured for the love of it. Continual bookwork stooped his back and wrecked his eyesight, but also gave him 'inexhaustible delight'. He was bringing Orpheus's teachings to Regency England, whether or not it cared.

Some 'liberal few', as he called them, approved of him. Ralph Waldo Emerson thought that reading his translations was like 'walking in the noblest of temples'. But this was a rare opinion. 'The man is an ass, in the first place,' cried 'The Literary Idler' in *Blackwood's Magazine*:

Secondly, he knows nothing of the religion of which he is so great a fool as to profess himself a votary; and, thirdly, he knows less than nothing of the language about which he is continually writing.

Some of this stung Taylor, largely self-taught as he was. But he insisted that he cared little for *words* and whether they were exactly correct, from the pedant's point of view. He cared about *things*: 'My efforts have been exerted to disseminate real wisdom, and not to amuse the inanities of folly.' To those who found Orphic philosophy a mere chaos, 'more wild than the delirious visions of Swedenborg, and more unconnected than the filthy rant of the stool-preaching methodist', he would reply that it was too beautiful for the sordid and base to understand.

He knew that any vestige of Orpheus's earth-life had gone, lost among 'immense ruins of time'. He admitted, in his (amended) preface to the hymns, that as many as four ancient versifiers, probably invented, laid claim to the sacred name and part of the mantle. He acknowledged, as one contemporary put it, that mythycists like Dupuis had 'argued the poet away . . . into a constellation'. But he did not doubt that Orpheus had truly lived, 'the first of prophets, and the prince of poets'.

And he was often near. At Lubbock's bank, where Taylor clerked for six years ('to some poor darkling desk confin'd'), the poet's music came through the high windows, danced in the dusty sun-motes, crept across the polished grilles. When Taylor went out, delivering bills around the City, Orpheus gleamed in the puddles, on the harness of the hackney carriages, and in the massing clouds:

Loud-sounding, lion-roaring, flashing fire,
In Air's wide bosom bearing thunders dire:
Impell'd by each sonorous stormy gale,
With rapid course along the skies ye sail.

Taylor had in any case perfected the 'philosophical death' in which, while the body was 'entomb'd' with letters of credit and interviewing of depositors, the soul was elsewhere. He knew how to walk with his friend, the *theologos*, in shining Greek meadows, while his body was on Ludgate Hill.

He would come home late and exhausted, Orpheus still in tow, to 9 Manor Place, a small rented house in the south London suburbs. He would take off his coat, boots and hat in the hall, greet his wife and children, eat a little, and then translate for hours. There was joking talk among the neighbours that 'Mr T' had sacrificed lambs in his lodgings, and poured out libations to Zeus, until the landlord had threatened to evict him. What was true was that ancient Greek was a lingua franca in the house, even at supper. Taylor, who had defiantly married very young, had taught his equally young wife to speak it. As they passed the *bekos* and the *gala*, bread and milk, and sipped their tea, Orpheus meditatively sipped along with them. His lyre, laid on the table, hummed with the draught that also stirred the curtains. Life-breathing winds, as he had sung and as Taylor knew, brought soul into the world and kept it aflame.

In Taylor's small study ('the abode of peace', according to Mary Wollstonecraft, who stayed with him for three months as a teenager), the Mysteries were once again unfolded. Orpheus sang, softly, from the shadows and the overburdened bookshelves, closing the gates of Taylor's senses and opening his mind to intelligible but ineffable worlds. Night was the time for initiation and re-creation. Taylor worked on, in the murky beam of an ordinary candle, while the divisions of wide Heaven and the circuits of the spheres opened up to him in the torchlight and incense of a Greek mountainside, and while passing pedestrians on Manor Lane, too late abroad, wondered what on earth the Philosopher of Walworth might be up to.

*

Behind Taylor's treasured scraps lay a revolution. The Greeks did not believe that men could emulate the gods; to do so was 'insolence'. To hope to become them was a step further, Dionysian madness. But Orpheus taught that it was possible, through ritual purity and sung, ecstatic prayer, to become one with the principles on which the universe was founded. It was not a matter of emulation or imitation. His followers were challenged to become what they already were. In words Rilke had heard from him before, *werde was du bist*, become what you are.

This principle was single. Though names and personalities filled Orpheus's theogony, all his goddesses were versions and virtues of the great Mother, all his gods were aspects of the creating and destroying power, and all these resolved to One: light, life, Love. The life-force that was Dionysus, scattered through the world, was one life; and soul in its many incarnations – from man, to beast, to bird – was one soul.

Music vibrated in everything, like the divine Breath or wisdom of Zeus through the air, and made all 'the things that are'; Orpheus, singing again, re-created and connected the world once more. *Each one separate, yet all things One.*

Some thought these secrets eventually killed him because they had been stolen from the gods, like the fire Prometheus had hidden in his fennel-stalk wand, and were too dangerous for humans to know. Orpheus's daring was epitomised, said Eratosthenes, by his habit of rousing himself to climb Mount Pangaion before dawn, just as the grey light was streaked with the slightest fire, before any other sleeper had stretched or stirred, to pray to the sun alone.

That mountain seemed the closest place he knew to home, the point to which he kept returning. Several peaks of the Rhodopes, though, may have seen those dawn ascents. The people of Plovdiv in Bulgaria feel certain he climbed Prayer Hill, a steep, rocky promontory above the old town where tourists dawdle among the painted houses. At its foot Orpheus is carved in concrete, singing by a stream, with votive beer bottles left beside him; halfway up, piano music drifts from the windows of the music academy; at the summit, littered with the scrawled-over ruins of several ancient citadels, the wooded mountains roll away south-wards and westwards in barricades of blue, while the whole Thracian plain lies bathed in northern light.

It is plausible that he was here. But the ancient Greeks believed that he went to Pangaion, as to his native place. He climbed quickly, expertly, through the low, holy oaks and the half-seen masses of the rocks. One hand held his lyre safe, the other bundled up his robes. At the summit was a mound like a mausoleum of large, squarish stones: a place where a king might lie, lifted up among the winds. He stood there, letting the breeze stir him, holding up his lyre to feel the opening vibrations of dawn steal through the strings. He watched for Helios-Apollo, the bright aureole of the sun, as Night faded slowly in the east and the birds fell silent at the first anticipation of light. Son sang to father, man to god, and musician to musician:

> Now in the quietness of star-strewn Night
> you watch the world. You bind it tight.
> Yours is the beginning, yours the unknown end,
> yours the growth and fading that the seasons send.
> From pole to pole with your resounding lyre
> you harmonise the world, now low, now higher:
> low notes for winter, high for summer's sun,
> Dorian mode for sweet spring to come . . .

Dorian was the mode of Dionysus, as well as his own. Pangaion held a sanctuary of the god, every part of which he knew: each carved-out altar and deep cistern, each wine-smelling grape press and libation channel, each hand-sized stoup in the marble rock from which he could scoop cold water to bless and bathe his face. He did so now, with stifled gasps, to make himself pleasing to the gods. The lower slopes were mined by several tribes for gold and silver, but at sunrise the workings were empty and the hammers quiet. Pangaion could be interpreted as 'all the world', encompassed in his gaze as Apollo held the universe in his own clear, infinite eye. Only mist lay beneath him, the smoking breath of the four white horses that drew the chariot of the untiring, swift-rushing, whip-cracking sun.

Almost imperceptibly, the sky was lightening. Stray clouds began to kindle and catch fire, red and gold, from the unseen source. *Dawn to the right,* he sang, *night to the left . . . Thou All of golden light, Thou All of ever-changing hues.* The sun's disc edged above the horizon, a stab of light that bit into the sky. The god was reborn. Orpheus was on his feet, his heart pounding and his arms outstretched to greet him. Helios had once allowed Phaeton to mount the chariot of the sun; and Orpheus in that height of desire might be swept up too, his veins shooting flame through his translucent limbs, scooped up in a net of light into the bursting, blinding day. There would be no more separation then; he would sublime, like the myrrh or frankincense that burned on his altars, into nothing but fragrance, music and fire. His song of it rushed now from Rilke's lips, urgently, softly: *Wolle die Wandlung. O sei für die Flamme begeistert —*

> *Will* transformation. Oh be inspired for the flame
> In which a thing disappears and bursts into something else;
> The spirit of re-creation which masters this earthly form
> Loves most the pivoting point where you are no longer
> yourself.

Light filled the whole sky now, a clear blue dome of day. The land still slept, the mountains purple-grey and the trees undifferentiated in darkness. A solitary wood-dove flew in silhouette across the scene, strangely quick against the slow, growing effulgence of the sun. But to him, as he gazed, far more than the visible sun blazed in this scene. Apollo transmitted the light of Zeus, who transmitted the light of Phanes in the furthest sphere of all. Phanes was Love, Zeus Mind, Apollo earthly creation vivified by both these things. The light of all three shone in splendour through the rays of the sun, the One made visible, though his roots were fixed beyond the starry-eyed darkness, incalculably deep and far.

On the island of Thynias Orpheus had stood among a crowd of heroes to salute Apollo, and had still been unable to look on his majesty flaming across the sky. Now, solitary, shivering in his cloak or suddenly wrapped in fire, he communed directly with him through the sun of mundane things. He was no longer orphaned. All things resolved to One. His own heart, the tuned and singing lyre, was the next mirror in which divine light shone.

The Jews of Alexandria, reviewing his story in the last centuries before Christ, presumed that his belief in one God was not accidental. (Orpheus was not strange to them; they painted him on the walls of their synagogues as a version of King David, playing his harp to the beasts in the wilderness.) Someone had taught him all the things he knew. And because the notion of one God seemed Hebraic rather than Greek, more ancient than the 'barbarian' Hellenic teachings by which they were surrounded, they assumed that his teacher had been Moses. There could be no other source.

Moses, of course, had also been in Egypt. He had been taught arithmetic, geometry, poetry, medicine and music, hieroglyphics and astronomy, to the highest Egyptian standards. He was enlightened, perfected, knew divine secrets. And he drew, beyond that, on the wisdom of Abraham. The young Thracian shaman and the Giver of the Law had possibly met there and talked together. Orpheus called him 'the one born of water', as though he had heard of the basket in the bulrushes.

A 'Testament of Orpheus', produced around the second century BC, claimed to be the poet's own work. He had seen the error of his ways; he no longer believed in multiple gods, and was transmitting his Mosaic lessons to his disciple Musaeus. The mood was secret, and dark:

> I shall speak to those entitled to hear it. Close the doors,
> all you profane! Listen,
> O Musaeus, child of the light-bearing moon,
> for I will declare what is true. Don't take the risk
> of losing eternity for your past opinions;
> but look to the divine word, apply yourself to it,
> keep true the inmost heart's receptacle
> of intellect, and tread the straight path well,
> perceive the single and eternal pattern,
> and only to the world's immortal king
> direct your gaze.
> He is one, self-proceeding; and from Him alone all things
>   proceed . . .
> Zeus, Hades, Helios, Dionysus, are one; one God in all.

Musaeus would not see this God, Orpheus told him. Abraham alone had achieved that, 'the only-begotten branch from the Chaldean tree'. And he, of course, had been a wondrous seer, 'knowing the course of the planets and how the spheres rotate on their axes around the earth'. But Orpheus vividly depicted, in words as fitting for Yahweh as for Zeus, the Creator-God that Moses had described to him, seated 'on a golden throne', making 'the hills' foundations quake' and his own limbs tremble. He controlled 'the winds of the air and the waters of the stream', as Orpheus too could do, channelling his power.

There were plausible echoes of Orpheus in this 'Testament'. Certain phrases – 'child of the light-bearing moon' (his tender term for his disciples), or 'the inmost heart's receptacle of intellect' – sounded like him. So did the secrecy. The whole testament was written, like 'his' hymns, in Greek hexameters – though hexameters, too, he was said to have got from Moses. Clement of Alexandria, coming to the 'Testament' as a new, proselytising Christian of the second century, treated it as genuine and useful, but pointed out that most of it was taken from someone else. Everything good in 'the Poet's' thinking, Clement wrote, had been borrowed from Isaiah, Amos, Deuteronomy, and Moses himself. In fact, and in general, the Greeks had cribbed all their best philosophy from the Jews. They had even stolen the idea of the pillars that, in some of their temples, represented the unknown God, for Moses had been guided by a pillar of fire in the desert.

Orpheus had also learned from Moses, Clement hinted, his habit of climbing holy mountains to meditate. He did not mean actual mountains, but 'the summit of intellectual things', from which others had to be debarred. (*'Close the doors, all you profane!'*) Alone, Orpheus entered the 'thick darkness', and there God was. Perhaps this was the meaning of the night journeys up Pangaion, as well as the ordeal underground. And perhaps, like Moses, he too returned to his disciples from these ascents – or descents – with his face shining, transfigured, knowing mysteries.

Given all this training, wrote Clement, it was no surprise that 'Orpheus the Thracian' sometimes sounded like a Jewish Patriarch. His song was not sufficiently divine, harmonised or holy; it came late, and he 'never sang it well enough'. But in some lines, sometimes, the tipsy young pagan was evidently grasping something:

> Deathless Immortal, uttered only to immortals,
> greatest of gods, with strong Necessity,
> dread, invincible and deathless one,
> whom Aether crowns . . .

> One Might, the great, the flaming heaven, was
> One Deity. All things one being were, in whom
> all these revolve: fire, water and the Earth.

The One God Orpheus sang of, as Proclus pointed out, was not really so familiar to Jews or Christians. He was male but also female, 'an immortal nymph'. He was 'the breath and form of all things, the source of Ocean, the movement in the undying fire'. He was the Beginning, because he created; the Middle, because he gathered creation back to him; and the End, because he embraced and annihilated whatever returned. Dancing shock-haired Shiva, the Creator-Destroyer of the Hindus, was much closer to what Orpheus meant than the God of the Jews. The blazing love-fire of all mystical traditions was nearer to his teachings than anything in the Pentateuch. But there was comfort for early Christians in the thought that the greatest singer of the Greeks had tamed the animals, moved the stones and harrowed Hell

with an 'echo', however faint and garbled, of what Abraham
had heard – and Moses, too.

From time to time, according to Apulian vase-painters of the
fourth century BC, Orpheus returned to the Underworld to
lead out to the astral plane the shadowy souls of women, men
and children. They may have been initiates in the Mysteries,
descending, like him, alive; they may have been the dead,
translated. He greeted them sometimes at the entrance to
Hades, holding back snarling Cerberus with one hand,
imparting secret passwords or formulas that would get them
safely through. He sang outside their tombs, intent and serious,
while they gripped small scrolls of his prayers as insurance.
At other times he performed his intercessions at Pluto's
portico, over the genteel chink of wine-cups, as he had done
before.

Instead of his lyre, he occasionally carried a shepherd's crook
to guide them. The souls crowned themselves with wreaths
of immortal laurel as he brought them, stumbling, back up
the path where Eurydice had vanished. He took them, too,
with his lyre, through the seven gates of the seven spheres,
interceding for them with the rulers he had met as he searched
for his lost love. And he escorted them at last to a place where
trees bowed over them and wild animals brushed gently past
them, the paradise-garden of his own singing, where they
could rest. Thus Rilke found himself, alive, astonished, among
the fountains and roses of Isfahan and Shiraz, gardens never
seen but now felt and recognised, where the figs ripened for
him and the singing breeze, moving between the branches,

almost became a face he knew.

In terracotta figurines, on rings interred with corpses and in medallions sewn on clothes, Orpheus was invoked as a rescuer and guide in the afterlife. In third- or fourth-century BC Thessaly, Italy and Crete his precise instructions for the journey, incised in his hexameters on paper-thin rolled gold leaves, were placed in the hands of the dead and buried with them. They included his prayer to bright-haired Persephone, 'that of her grace she send me to the seats of the hallowed', and the formula 'Now, on this day, you have died and come to life'. Those who held these foil scraps were excused further births and dissolutions. Such trust in his power to win souls immortality was by then many centuries old. Bone sacrificial tokens of the fifth century BC from Olbia, on the northern shore of the Black Sea, were scratched with his name and four words that summed up everything: 'Life: Death: Life. – Truth'.

His adventures, too, gave comfort. Terracotta vases showed him outsinging the Sirens, though their music wrapped death around him. In tomb frescoes and reliefs into the late imperial years he was shown pleading for Eurydice and leading her into the light. He was preserved, as he had to be, on the point of success. Only more secular or self-confident ages preferred to stress that he had failed.

After the coming of Christianity, Orpheus the soul-saver haunted the catacombs and the houses of the dead. A particularly striking image was painted in the fourth century AD in the cemetery of the Two Laurels in Rome. Orpheus solemnly faced the viewer from a tympanum, dressed in long robes, with lyre and plectrum held in his outstretched hands as iconic and holy things. His attendant animals had been reduced to the only two that mattered: the dove of peace, quiescent, to his right, and the hook-beaked, soul-carrying eagle to his left. His place among the tombs was not decorative, but vital. He had become a saviour; in fact, though he still wore his floppy Thracian cap, he had become Christ.

It happened elsewhere. By late Antiquity his image, carved on amulets or gemstones to protect against the evil eye, was sometimes marked with a Christian cross to keep the wearer extra-safe. Crosses were added to mosaics of him to make them magical or holy. In exchange, Christ was given his own seven stars. One haematite amulet of the third or fourth century, last seen in pre-war Berlin before it disappeared, showed Orpheus (identified by the inscription) hanging on the cross, with the crescent moon and stars above him. His lyre became a symbol on Christian seals, together with the fish and the dove. Alexander Severus, a third-century Roman emperor, was said to have placed a statue of Orpheus in his *lararium*, his household shrine to the protecting gods. He rubbed shoulders there with other 'very sacred souls': Abraham, Apollonius of Tyana, Christ.

He was very seldom worshipped, only invoked as a man who knew the secrets of the afterlife and could bring healing and peace. But for four centuries, in popular iconography, he and Christ regularly changed places. Christians, like the Greeks before them, found him a popular authority for the truths they were trying to promote, a way in to the new religion for those who felt unsure. Orpheus too, like Jesus, had a divine father, drew disciples to hard lives in wild places, preached of original sin, eternal rewards and punishments, and acted as a bridge between the invisible divine and men: 'the gods' interpreter', as Horace called him. If Christ was the *logos*, Orpheus had been the Word's first, far-distant singing. He too evoked the Vine, with his followers as branches.

He also harrowed Hell, and sometimes drew souls out of it. Most spectacularly, in Calderón's *El divino Orfeo* of 1634, he thrust his *arpa-cruz*, his holy lyre, in Pluto's face and appeared, in Hell in glory, improbably nailed to the cross. Yet because he was a pagan he usually failed at this, as Christ could not. How close he might have come to the truths of Christian doctrine, some Church fathers exclaimed, with just a little more effort and more thought! His 'Testament', widely cited by early Christian writers, showed him on the right track, though his embrace of monotheism went along with a worryingly constant devotion to Dionysus; he had coated the cup-rim with honey, wrote one, but the drink in his cup was poison all the same.

By the fifth century the Church, confident and strong, did not need to lean on Orpheus any more. Yet his identification with Jesus lingered in the iconography. He was the Good Shepherd, shown increasingly with sheep only, or with lambs that lay down beside lions. (One of 'his' lost books had been called *The Good Shepherd*, undoubtedly meaning himself.) In that same Calderón *auto* he was a shepherd as well as a god, addressed by Eurydice as 'Pastor', and promising her as she sank away from him, overwhelmed by the mists of the lower world, that he would continue to appear before her in the chalice and the Host.

Clement of Alexandria deserves the last word. Though he

had seen him both drunk and disorderly, he seems also to have met him quietly intent on his music, in the woods; though he denied that Orpheus had ever tamed or saved anyone, he linked him with Christ as a singer who tuned the discord of the elements, 'so that the whole world might become harmony'.

And then there was the matter of how he died.

Jean Delville, *Orpheus*, 1893

Seventh string: Scattering

His killers were the women of Thrace. For three years he had stolen their men from them for occult instruction they could not share, and had also shunned all female contact. Possibly he had promised Eurydice he would never marry again; possibly, too, he had not yet recovered from that love and that despair. In Ovid's *Metamorphoses* he sang viciously of women changed into flints. He too was now flint-hearted.

He climbed to the high shrines with male companions only, or sat among the rocks alone. Girls ventured near him, left milk or cakes as offerings to the beautiful musician, and slipped away through the trees. He paid no attention. Cocteau's Orpheus was assailed by schoolgirls who mobbed him, demanded his autograph, pawed at his clothes. '*Lâche moi!*' he cried, despairingly. *Leave me alone.* A tender touch or a doe-eyed look could no longer affect him; a hand stroking his dark curls, under the knotted laurel, did nothing for him:

For nothing is worse or more shameful than woman.

Pygmalion too, in Orpheus's 'telling' of the story, had scorned women 'and the many faults implanted in them'. In his case the phase was temporary. Orpheus's seemed longer-lasting. In so far as he sought human comfort, he now loved Calais, the son of the wolf-cloaked north wind, who had sailed with him on board the *Argo*: a boy with dark wings feathered like the Thracian snow, and whose small red lips were cold as frost.

Did it matter that Orpheus loved him? Ovid said he introduced homosexual practices among the Greeks, seeking out tender boys and 'plucking the first blooms'. In the deep groves, Orpheus sang out his desire for Calais, just as he had sung his love for Eurydice years before. Yet almost every god in Orpheus's pantheon was both male and female, throbbing with love and generative power. The poet, as creator, needed to combine male and female in himself. And Apollo too had loved boys, especially Hyacinthus. He had desired him so crazily, 'beyond all other mortals', that he put on hunter's skins and strode through the woods, arrows forgotten, lyre cast away, just to stay with him. They ran with the hounds together, laid out nets. After the hunt they stripped in the noonday heat and oiled each other, golden god and gilded boy.

Ovid's Orpheus sang the song of Apollo's courtship, and its sudden end. In the meadows one day, half-tussling, half-loving, the pair threw the discus together. The god, too eager to impress, hurled the bronze disc 'until its weight scattered the clouds' and it bounced back to strike Hyacinthus, killing him. In a second he was cold, grey, limp, red blood gushing from his face. He died 'like violets in a garden'. Apollo, death-pale and desperate, stroked and anointed the body again as if he could arouse him. He rubbed herbs on Hyacinthus, Orpheus sang, to stop the spirit leaving: a cure he himself might have tried, perhaps, on that awful morning in the long, green, unfeeling grass.

The god's efforts had no effect. But they did not cease because the boy had died. Apollo wept over him, transformed him into the larkspur flower that bowed and blew on the hillside, inscribed his own cries of sorrow on those dark-blue petals. Orpheus, gently picking them, touched his father's tears: *Ai, ai*, as piercing as when they first fell. All Apollo's songs thenceforth were laments for his boy lover. Was that wrong? As Orpheus sang of Apollo – and as Ovid, at that fatal moment in Hades, had sung of him – what could he be blamed for, except for love?'

Medieval Orpheus, too, was sometimes declared innocent of blame for abandoning women. Giovanni del Virgilio reported that, after his journey to Hell, Orpheus renounced temptation and turned instead to God. The world no longer delighted him; he became a monk or a hermit, possessing Eur-dike in the form of Wisdom and desiring nothing else.

Increasingly, in any version of his life, he was alone. Often he chose to be. But seventeenth-century writers saw him as the poet at the peak of his tragedy and melancholy, rejected by society, attacked by the unfeeling world. The Romantic poets recognised him all too well, misunderstood and exiled: 'torn in pieces', by the reviewers, as Shelley anticipated. Cocteau saw himself in Orpheus, no longer esteemed or thought relevant by a post-war literary world that had moved away from surrealism and his dreams. An anonymous letter from Orpheus's enemies at the Café des Poètes, 'the centre of the world', announced what his fate would be.

He was singing in his solitude when the Thracian women

found him and took their revenge. Again he was on Pangaion, with the world around him. He was in a temple, Konon said, though most artists placed him in his usual sanctuary, the trees. The season was autumn, as it had to be. Red-figure Attic wine-bowls, ready to brim with blood pressed from the vine and the dismembered god, showed him in his shaman's robes as the murderers appeared. His Thracian-warrior acolytes were already shrinking back.

Some said Dionysus himself had dispatched these women, the frenzied Maenads of Orpheus's earlier life. The god was displeased with his reforms and his Apollonian ways. The Maenads ran towards him with tattooed arms raised to strike, shrieking the chants of the rites he had supplanted. Others thought Aphrodite played a part in it, taking revenge for a slight from Calliope, his mother, by making these women love him until they tore him apart. He was a young man still, armed only with his lyre. His killers wore skins and carried hunting spears.

Strabo thought this catastrophe had been building for some time. Orpheus had got above himself, acquired a rabble of followers and tried to grab power. His enemies there-fore 'suspected a plot and violence, so they combined against him and destroyed him'. Pausanias agreed. Though the Greeks believed 'many untruths' about Orpheus, including the idea that his mother was Calliope and that he had gone down to Hades alive, he had 'in my opinion' reached a pinnacle of power because of his cures, his mystical teach-ings and the beauty of his songs. From that pinnacle he had to fall.

He was killed, too, because he was different: for what he

taught and knew, for how he loved. The many ancient paint-ings of the murder scene (a favourite theme in the Athenian Golden Age) always showed him as a stranger, though he was in his own country. The Orpheus who was killed was not Thracian, but Greek. He sometimes wore nothing but a cloak round his shoulders and a gold thread round his hair, the prettily, uselessly braided ringlets cascading down his back. This made his death worse: the civiliser torn apart by barbar-ians, and the nude, vulnerable man destroyed by the clothed and the armed. Yet often the painted vases showed only farmers' wives attacking him. Possibly they were drunk too, like the Maenads, giving themselves courage first. They seized whatever they had to hand – pots and pans, pestles, spits – as they might have driven off a wandering beggar from their doors. They hurled stones to cast out the polluted one, though he was pure.

At the first blow he fell to one knee, raising his lyre to protect himself. He never thought to snatch up stones in his own hands. Song was his defence. The women levelled their long spits or spears to drive them into his singing, heaving chest, but music could fend off pain. Ovid saw him with both arms outstretched as he had stretched them towards Eurydice, seemingly imploring death to retreat from him, grabbing for the ghost of life. Charmed birds still beat about him until they were knocked, bloody and broken, out of the sky. Virgil said he went on singing and playing and that his notes, from his plectrum's sweeping glissandi in the air, for a time repelled the stones and spears and made them swerve away. As they touched lyre, or heart, their sharpness softened, as it always had. One stone, wrote

Ovid, even as it was thrown, 'was conquered by the harmon-ious song of voice and lyre and, like a suppliant asking pardon for such deeds of furious violence, fell before his feet'.

Rilke, battered and bleeding, urged him on: *du Göttlicher, du Schöner*.

> you, divine one, till the end still sounding . . .
> outsounded their cries with order, beautiful one,
> from among the destroyers arose your upbuilding song.

Whenever he faltered in that song a missile smashed into his body and the knife of a woman's scream twisted after it, while a cacophony of horns and drumming beat him sense-less by sound alone, as he knew it could. Cornets and oboes, the Furies' sounds, opened long, gaping vents in his flesh. Cocteau added screaming whistles and kettle drums. His sinews were wrenched apart, his bones snapped, his limbs disjointed. Red welled from the pegs of his lyre, dripped from the golden strap; gushed from his breast. Dissonance destroyed him until he fell to the ground, bleeding music. Ovid remarked that it was like a morning in the arena.

Yet in the end he was ready for transformation. He had learned through Eurydice the patience of love and the openness of death. The sacrifice of the body, though inevitably he clung to it, was a small exchange for resurrection into higher life. Anouilh's Orpheus had gone obediently and quietly to the place of his death, a hill near an olive grove, where he had waited in his overcoat in the night chill for everything to be 'pure and clear and luminous', and for Eurydice to be once more in his arms. 'If you find her,' Death told him, 'you find yourself.' Cocteau's Orpheus, feeling the first stones wound him, cried that he understood now what marble felt when it was chipped, cut and split into a masterpiece: 'Life is sculpting me, Heurtebise. Let it finish its work.' With open arms this time, he turned to the other side.

The death-blow came from the sacred double-axe, the tree-feller. It cleaved him so that life and voice were 'breathed out into the winds'. Orpheus in this scene was again a vegetation god, cut down because the seasons demanded harvest, pressing and winnowing to release new life. He was broken and spread out by hoes, mattocks, rakes and bloodied hands. This was Dionysus's death, or a foreshadowing of Christ's. The holy man does not dance, Sufis say, until he dances in his own blood.

Bacon saw his death as a metaphor for the history of the world. Wisdom prevailed awhile, but men became depraved again; kingdoms fell, and barbarism returned. Learning and philosophy 'must needs be dismembered, so that a few fragments only in some places will be found'. Those fragments, Orpheus's life, now shone scarlet on the bushes or hung, as one fifteenth-century writer saw them, like bloody rags through the woods. In the autumnal Rhodopes they still flare out, red leaves of dogwood or sycamore among the pines. The small pink-lobed *silivriak*, too, the 'Orpheus-flower', which grows on the cliffs by the Trigradska river, is taken for his blood.

It was right that he should be killed at sunset, the last intense gathering of colours towards the dark. The many flowed back to the One, and sounds to silence. The flat round sun, sinking and reddening like unleavened bread, shone on the blue-and-crimson plain of his scattering, later to whiten and glisten under the earth-splitting frost.

Diogenes Laertius, pleased to be contrary, thought lightning killed him. Zeus had sent 'heavenly fire' to destroy Orpheus because of the mysteries he had revealed. If so, Orpheus had already sung that heart-stopping horror:

> Holy and invincible, suddenly crashing down,
> an endless spiral of noise, omnivorous in its dive,
> unbreakable, threatening, ineluctable; the gale's
> sharp and smoke-filled shaft swoops down –

He had petitioned instead for 'a sweet end', and 'divine peace'. Fate, his own song-breath, determined otherwise. Plato, too, said that his death served Orpheus right, because of his cowardly refusal to die to recover the Beloved. Love demanded, and should have been given, everything.

As that fatal evening drew in, creation wept over him. The trees bowed down in grief; sapless, their twigs broke as though they had no life in them. Their leaves folded, withered and fell to the stone-strewn pathways of his woods. Songless, like him, the birds flew heavily under the lowering clouds, and the fowls of the water closed their wings across their misting eyes. His silver rivers were now salt tears, running brackish through brown wild mint and reeds. The withered stalks and flower-stems trailed and trembled, lyres unstrung. The death of Orpheus brought winter, with no certainty of spring.

Antipater of Sidon wrote his epitaph:

No more, Orpheus, shalt thou lead the charmed oaks and rocks and the shepherdless herds of wild beasts. No more shalt thou will to sleep the howling winds and the hail, and the drifting snow, and the roaring sea . . .

Why sigh we for our dead sons, when not even the gods have the power to protect their children from death?

His head and lyre, flung into the Hebrus – nailed together, said Phanocles – were carried down to the shore. The head, though grey as stone on its ragged neck, was still alive. It bled into the water. Lucian was sure it sang a funeral dirge, while the lyre seemed to ring and resound with the wind's slow creep among the strings. Ovid, as if tired of the tragedy, heard only 'something tearful, I don't know what': *flebile nescio quid*. Virgil heard the ice-cold tongue murmur and sing 'Eurydice! ah, poor Eurydice!', with the low banks answering:

> *Eurydicen vox ipsa et frigida lingua*
> *a miseram Eurydicen! anima fugiente vocabat,*
> *Eurydicen toto referebant flumine ripae.*

Within the flux of earthly generation, the swirl of the river, Orpheus was reduced to love and defined by it; there was nothing else. As Rumi said, 'Love plays and plays, and is the music played.' As Night, his cooling nurse, spread out across the clouds, head and lyre were borne on the floodtide towards sea and ocean and the pull of the horizon-brimming sky. Naiads and dryads escorted them, their water-garments black as kelp and their loose hair shaken out in sorrow.

Meanwhile, in Thrace, the weeping Muses gathered up his bones and flesh in remembrance. They searched for him among the deaf and unmoving stones. Calliope led them, sobbing loudest, her white robes stained and muddied with the chaff of her son. But, as Milton whispered, what good could that have done?

> What could the Muse her self that *Orpheus* bore,
> The Muse her self for her inchanting son
> Whom Universal nature did lament . . .

A few of the Maenads, too, crept back to his killing field. These also helped to gather him. Afterwards, desperate to cleanse themselves of his blood, they tried to bathe in the Helicon, the river of his inspiration. But Aeschylus said the river promptly dived underground for twenty-two *stadia*, or four miles, shaking them off and emerging different, uninvolved, crystal-pure, with another name. Something of Orpheus survived in that flowing and that escape. He was preserved too in the Hebrus, in flecks of gold and in a strange, bewitching, unguent property of the water. Girls came there to dip their delicate hands in it and wash their thighs.

The Maenads, amazed, watched the Helicon as it sank. But as they stood their toes began to grip, dig and curl; they grew hard, fissured bark, sprouted terror-branches from their necks, felt their scrawny legs pulled and twisted like the grey pine-roots that writhed from rocks on Orpheus's mountains, until they were hag-trees heaped across each other. The river laughed as it disappeared.

Yet vengeance, if that was what it was, was unnecessary. Orpheus was bound to return. The child Dionysus, dismembered by the Titans, was revived with every spring. The Orpheus-flower, when it has been dried and pressed for thirty days in paper, may still be planted: it lives and grows, and opens its petals to the pale light of the gorge.

The poet, too, by making many descents, suffering many deaths, ever changing and transforming, would achieve immortality. Orpheus's voice went on being heard precisely because the Maenads had scattered him. He had entered Nature, whispered Rilke from the buds and leaves; he has entered us.

> But they finally tore you apart, those maddened avengers,
> while yet the sound of you lingered in lions and boulders,
> lingered in birds and in trees, where you still sing today.
>
> Only because you were butchered in terrible anger
> – O you lost God! O divine, indestructible trace! –
> Are *we* ears that can hear and a mouth for what Nature can
> say.

*

That divine trace is not always obvious. But you may begin to find it in a glade in a wood that grows along a hillside, somewhere in the south-west of England. A weak winter sun shines into it, but it is thoroughly filled with silent forms and shade. Old hawthorns and birches people it. Dead webs make up its structure: brambles growing skywards, ivy dangling to earth, stem-nets wrapped around the bases of the trees. More ivy clusters in the canopy, so thickly you might almost believe that summer leaves are growing there. But it is too dark, too brutal, a crumpled blanket from which the birds have fled.

You recognise this as a Dionysian scene. The trees are the

bacchoi, shadowy, garlanded and slightly stooped, as though they listen. Their naked trunks gleam in the cold; their *thyrsoi* are the ivy vines. One beech is caught, arms and breasts uplifted, her bare branches sweeping behind her. A Maenad tree, with others following. At their feet lies a cushioning pelt of debris and dead leaves that smells of sweat, sweet rot and fermentation, like the press of the wine god. Gouts of bright blood still hang along the wire fence and on the thorns. That sighing in the air may still be '*Evoi! Evoi!*' echoing from the hill, or the dancers' exhausted gasps as they rotate, whirl slower, collapse and disappear, from thought as well as life.

Yet these are not the only signs of Orpheus in this landscape. Music plays, even here. Thomas Hardy knew how to hear it. The treble, tenor and bass of the wind, varying with the irregularities of the land; the 'baritone buzz' of a holly tree; the thinner, local, papery sound, 'a worn whisper', of the hundreds of mummified heath-bells of last summer. Thorn bushes whistle in a mournful key, but the tone of a pollard thorn is higher, as the wind rushes through its stiff twigs like water through a sieve. Tits and warblers give a treble line, with the great tit the most insistent, like an unoiled gate, or like a creaking door that will open eventually from winter into Orpheus's spring.

To his song, the seasons change. On a late-summer hillside that rock is his singing seat, under the hallowing larches; wheatear and wagtail fly to his rhythm; the bent-grass quivers, the bee plunders the gleaming rock-rose, at his direction. The bracken slope is laced and strung with new growth like a lyre catching the light. Stones in a dry wall, or pebbles on a path, wait for his notes to transform them like the bright running-down of the rain. That rain too, percussive and soft, sings differently on the crimson-backed swags of the copper beech, the green-fingered ash, or the willow pricked with gold in the mists of a September evening. The whole world buzzes, shines and blows with him, sending back the song: in Rilke's words, *such saying as never the things themselves / hoped so intensely to be.*

Under Orpheus's gaze there is nothing entirely silent, or quite still. And there is nothing dead that has not passed into some deeper, more splendid being, as Eurydice had shown him long ago: fallen, distributed, given away. In his own dissolution he had found Wisdom, learned Love, changed at last into himself: become life.

*

At Lesbos, off the coast, his head and lyre were washed up on the sand. Supposedly they were found by a fisherman, who used the lyre's gold strap to pull them from the water. He noted with astonishment that the head was still singing, undamaged by the sea, 'blooming and bleeding with fresh blood'. A gold thread still tied back the dark, lustrous curls. As the head lay there, helpless and dripping with foam, a savage snake struck and spat at it. In slow coils, its scales glistening, it circled the head until Apollo turned the creature to stone. The snake was Time, rebuffed from its usual destructive work; the head, like the fame of all great poets, was bound to go on singing.

The lyre, enshrining divinity and intellect, was hung up in

Apollo's temple, where breezes could still stir it. The head, representing the senses, was stowed in a cave of Dionysus or in a cleft of the earth, where it gave continual prophecies, oracles and healing. Trees grew from it, blown by a wind that was not felt elsewhere. People came from as far as Babylon to consult it. Cyrus, King of Persia, heard it prophesy his conquests. Aristaeus, the would-be seducer of Eurydice, heard it cry out for revenge against him as it killed his swarm of bees. But the head was placated with a sacrifice of oxen, out of whose charred bodies a new trail of golden bees buzzed and flew like lyre-notes: sweetness from putrefaction, life out of death.

The survival of the head also signified the persistence of Orpheus on earth. Death, it seemed, had agreed not to claim him. Cocteau's Orpheus was released by his Death completely, though she still loved him. Shot dead in his struggle with the avant-garde Bacchantes, he had returned to her; but she ordered him killed again in the Underworld, in order to revive him on Earth's terms. There had to be many deaths. He went back, buffeted and blown by *une grande souffle inexplicable*, through the softly reassembling mirror to the earth-mire he had left. The road lay open between death and life, the truth and the lie. Orpheus now forgot all he had learned and left on the other side; his bourgeois life resumed. But the poet lived, one day to make melodies again.

An Attic cup showed the severed head with its eyes open, thrown back to sing as when it had thrilled the Thracian shepherds, while a young scribe with his tablet on his knee carefully took down the words. But Apollo grew jealous of this rival to his own oracle. He ordered it to 'cease from the things that are mine' and added, according to Philostratus, 'I've put up with your singing long enough.' Indeed there had been many, many songs.

The head immediately ceased to prophesy, as a son to his father's command. It did not necessarily cease to sing. Poets and artists imagined that it went on, defying critics and reviewers as well as death. In 1993 *The Sandman* graphic version placed it in a charnel house during Robespierre's terror, where, glowing blue-white among its severed fellows, it sang of tyranny overthrown, of liberty and love. Around it, the other heads came alive and joined in.

Yet this remnant of Orpheus, living but helpless, longed to die. Enshrined again after the French Revolution in a temple on a Greek island, it waited for its father Morpheus, god of dreams, to impose silence as Apollo had done. More centuries passed. In the end, in five brutal frames, blue-cloaked Morpheus kissed the head, snapped its life-thread and closed its staring eyes. Fresh scarlet blood soaked his arms and dripped to the ground, where it flowered. Morpheus shrugged the incident away. Orpheus, after all, had died many times before.

Under a cherry tree the head was buried deep. Those who buried it, teenagers only half-aware what it was, were unsure whether Orpheus's spirit had gone to Elysium or nothingness. But perhaps it would rise into the cherry tree, 'and in spring the new blossoms will be his, and in summer the cherries will taste of true poetry and song'. And those close to death, gently fed with that sweetness, would be young again.

Meanwhile the lyre in the temple, as if it was Orpheus's beating heart preserved from his dispersing, softly filled Lesbos with the germ of all lyric song, both tunes and words. It became the last place, after Paros, Samos and Samothrace, to hear his Mysteries directly. Phanocles thought that local people buried head and lyre in a tomb on the shore, from where music continued to flow out over the bitter blue-green sea that had borne them there.

The lyre was stolen once. The son of Pittacus the tyrant fell in love with it, and bribed Apollo's priest to exchange it for another. Afraid to play it openly in the city, he took it outside the walls at night, hidden under his cloak. But the sounds he made were so raw and tuneless that only the wild dogs gathered, and tore him apart. Without Orpheus, or Apollo's shining benediction, the magic lyre was no more musical than ordinary string and shell.

Traditionally Orpheus was buried first at Libethra, in the foothills of Mount Olympus. His shattered bones were placed in a stone urn on a pillar, set within a fence in a grove of his sacred oaks. Women were not allowed there. Ever afterwards, Thracians claimed, the nightingales that nested and fledged on his tomb sang louder and more sweetly than elsewhere. Night brimmed over with them.

Some made sacrifices to him there, revering him as a god. But his story was always much too human; and the bones, in any case, were eventually moved away. Pausanias heard a tale in Larissa that a shepherd, dozing at noon by Orpheus's pillar among the oak trees, spontaneously began to sing the poet's songs in a loud, sweet voice. (Sleeping here was as dangerous as under apple trees, open to bewitchment.) Other shepherds and herdsmen gathered round him, pushing and shoving to see the sleeper who sang, until the pillar was overturned and the urn broken. This brought down a flood that destroyed Libethra, and Orpheus's bones were therefore moved to the fortified city of Dium, in Macedonia. This was a centre for the worship of many gods, including Zeus and Dionysus. A tumulus, locals say, still marks the spot where Orpheus is buried. In ancient times it bore an epitaph, saying that he had been killed by lightning.

Across the border, however, some Bulgarian archaeologists think his tomb is at Tatul near Kardzhali, a semicircular niche in a rock mound on top of a mountain. It dates, perhaps, from the second millennium BC. Artefacts found there in 2004 – clay altars and tools of semi-precious stones, channels for libations, the remains of a solar clock – suggest that this was a pilgrimage site where the sun god was once worshipped. A tiny bronze statuette of a lyre-player with a plectrum in his right hand hints at a cult of Orpheus, or his burial place. He might have been laid there, above ground, like the Thracian king he was.

Certainly visitors believe it. They file down the new concrete path to clamber over the difficult rocks, boyfriends hauling up girlfriends to recline provocatively in the semicircular tomb, down which, some say, wine or blood once ran in streams. At the holy well beside it, they toss in coins. The coach-park is still a farmyard where black hens peck the dust and an old Pomak woman, in Turkish scarf and trousers, walks slowly past with firewood. Her sunburned, wizened husband gazes shyly from the half-open gate. They have no water here; the maize has been baked brittle, and the ground is hard. But he has placed his worn wicker chair to take offerings just where the coach parties disembark. He, too, waits for Orpheus to transform this scene like rain.

In the ancient world memorials multiplied. In Memphis a life-size votive statue of Orpheus was put up, around 300 BC, in the Hemicircle of the Poets. A century later a stone and brass image, picked out in gold, was raised in the sanctuary of the Muses on Mount Helicon. He stood beside a figure called Telete, 'Initiation', in his long priest's robes and a pointed Persian cap. Bronze animals surrounded him. Around AD 240 Philostratus the younger, the connoisseur of paintings, saw this 'most beautiful' statue, or imagined he had:

> It was adorned with a Persian tiara spangled with gold and rising high from his head, and a chiton hanging from his shoulders to his feet was cinched at the breast by a golden belt. His hair was so luxuriant and so instinct with the spirit of life as to deceive the senses into thinking it was being tossed and shaken by gusts of wind – for the hair behind on the neck fell free down the back, while the parted hair which lay above the eyebrows gave a full view of the pure glance of his eyes. His sandals shone brightly with the yellowest gold, and his robe fell ungirded down his back to his ankles; and he was carrying his lyre . . . For the bronze even acted the part of the strings . . . almost indeed becoming vocal and producing the very sound of the notes.

At Orpheus's feet, below the gazing animals, 'you could see the bronze taking on the shape of rivers flowing from their sources towards the singing, and a wave of the sea raising itself aloft for love of the song'.

On the Esquiline Hill in first-century Rome, just where

you pulled up breathless after the climb from Subura (Martial said), the poet was carved in white marble and became a dripping, sparkling water-feature, a public fountain encircled by animals slaking their thirst with his music. Three churches – S. Agata, S. Martino and S. Lucia 'in Orfea' – still preserve his name there. In Roman-occupied Plovdiv in the second century someone carved his name, in 'his' Cyrillic letters, all along the tenth row of the eastern section of the new amphitheatre. He is remembered in stone or bronze in modern Stockholm, Florence, Leeds and Providence, Rhode Island; he floats, in bright bronze spars, from the ceiling of the Lincoln Center in New York. In Smolyan in the Rhodopes, at the foot of a sheer cliff called 'Orpheus's rocks', he sings to Eurydice in the market-place and, in front of the theatre, leads her out of Hell. And on a mountain north of Kardzhali his statue, paid for by the Rotary Club, was unveiled in 2005 by the mayor and district governor with balloons and a fly-past and the local high-school majorettes. As they strutted and twirled, Orpheus remained absorbed in the music of his own heart.

Indeed there was no point, Rilke wrote – was made to write – in tombs, urns or memorials. *Errichtet keinen Denkstein.*

> *Laßt die Rose*
> *nur jedes Jahr zu seinen Gunsten blühn.*
> *Denn Orpheus ists. Seine metamorphose*
> *in dem and dem. Wir sollen uns nicht mühn*
> *um andre Namen. Ein für alle male*
> *ists Orpheus, wenn es singt. Er kommt und geht.*

Raise no commemorating stone. The roses

shall blossom every summer for his sake.
For this is Orpheus. His metamorphosis
in this one and in that. We should not take

thought about other names. Once and for all,
it's Orpheus when there's singing. He comes and goes.

He had no fixed place or monument, for he was in every-thing that flowed, grew or changed. With Eurydice-Persephone, he had entered the mystery of life and death. He was the glow that suffused the petals of the roses on Rilke's summer writing desk, or the flame-vermilion that stained them; their silk-soft translucence, like a cambric dress, in the morning light through the window; their porcelain opalescence in the warming air. And isn't it enough, the air murmured, *Ists nicht schon viel*,

if sometimes he can dwell
with us a few days longer than a rose?

Petals dropping on the table from the rose-bowl still held his music in their perfume, their light, and in the careless beauty of their separation; withered, crimsoned, pressed in paper, they still sang. *He comes and goes* – from life to death, death to life. As the Olbia tokens had proclaimed twenty-five centuries earlier (but there is no time with him, they are fresh-scratched now):

Life: Death: Life. – Truth.

Nonetheless, he was often confined to a Heaven of some kind. Several travellers glimpsed him in the rose-tinged 'ampler aether' of the Elysian Fields, where they presumed his shade had gone. A brighter, particular sun and stars shone on the groves and meadows there. Gluck heard him singing ecstatically, softly, in a manner as simple and unaffected as birdsong, of the quality of the light:

Che puro ciel

Che chiaro sol

Che nuova serena luce

E questa mai!

Polygnotos painted him on a hill there, still sitting alone, leaning against a willow tree to learn more songs. Virgil spotted him in his long trailing robes in the midst of happy dancers and naked wrestlers, 'matching their measures with the seven clear notes', striking the strings with his fingers 'and sometimes with an ivory quill'. Others reported him united there with Eurydice, 'daring now to turn and smile at her', as Ovid gently said. Milton saw him asleep on a bed of heaped Elysian flowers, lifting his head only to hear 'soft *Lydian* Aires':

Such as the meeting soul may pierce

In notes, with many a winding bout

Of linkèd sweetness long drawn out . . .

Untwisting all the chains that ty

The hidden soul of harmony.

Dante, with Virgil as his guide, encountered Orpheus in Limbo, the first circle of Purgatory for the virtuous unbaptised, walking in a meadow of enamelled green in a 'high, luminous place' with Cicero, Seneca and Horace.

Yet Elysium would not in any case have been the end, for him. It merely marked a pause until he could say these words, 'most truly' and 'sincerely':

I have paid the penalty for deeds unrighteous

whether Fate laid me low or the Gods Immortal . . .
I have flown out of the sorrowful, weary circle,
and stepped, swift-footed, on the circle of joy.

In his prospectus in the *Argonautica* he had included 'the
courses of the stars'. Thracian priests were said to know 500
heavenly bodies by their names. During his night rituals, or
walking in the dark alone, he ardently observed them. Both
Night and Dionysus wore them like a robe, and each one
housed a demon. These eternal fires, watching, joyous, whirling
in his usual spinning-top circles, were 'the source of everything below'. And the fire-part of him, too, once loosed for
good from existence, would join the circuits of the stars. The
flames of his praise, as sung at sea and on the mountains,
would light the universe then.

In time his lyre was set there. The Muses, having found no
one on earth who could emulate him, asked Zeus to place it
in heaven as a new constellation. The god sent an eagle to
retrieve it, and this too became fixed in the firmament, wings
folded and eye fierce. Aquila and Lyra blazed together: though
the lyre, without Orpheus's fine, strong, long-fingered hands,
played only in the imaginations of beasts and men.

In 1915 Edward Thomas, staring heavenwards, began to
form what was, perhaps, his first poem:

> This is the constellation of the lyre:
> Its music cannot ever tire,
> For it is silent. No man need fear it:
> Unless he wants to, he will not hear it.

It was said that the animals of the Zodiac still circled round

Lyra, and that the gods tethered their chariots, pausing to listen, in that part of Heaven. In summer it shone directly overhead, nailed to the night by dazzling Vega like a diamond, blue and white.

Rilke's Vera also seemed to hear it. Before illness stopped her, she would dance slowly in circles and on tiptoe, raising her white arms to make a tree that seemed to become, for one brief moment, a constellation of points of light. She danced to a music only she could discern, moving for the sake of the invisible poet who played it, and only for him.

But Orpheus himself was not yet ready to live among the stars. Though his life-spark had been scattered through the earth as if in valediction, his soul was still not purified enough to leave. Indeed, said Plato, still censorious, the gods refused to honour him with permanent heaven. And so, after a thousand years had passed, he found himself again in the Field of Asphodel in Hades, lining up to drink.

Since he came this time from Elysium, the way looked different. His perception was pure now, cleansed to the elemental soul-view of the other side of life. Rather than crossing the gloomy marsh of Cocytus, he descended to a meadow full of pink-white shining flowers and crowded, as Virgil described it, with souls robed in white, 'like bees on a sunny day, when gleaming white lilies are scattered everywhere'. This was the chasm where Dionysus had walked once in the other world, feeling his soul grow heavy with liquefaction and the desire to be born again. Orderly and quiet, in long procession, the souls lined up to drink Lethe's water and return 'beneath the vault of the sky'.

There was an alternative, Orpheus dimly remembered (but

the memory faded as fast as he moved forward, along with the brightness of the light). It was important to be careful of the branching paths, and to keep to the right 'as far as you can go'. He had to look out for the poplar trees. The water should be ice-cold, colder surely than this. The guardians of the holy right-hand spring would surely give it to him. He had not forgotten the words:

> I am a child of Earth and starry Heaven;
> But my race is of Heaven alone, and you know it.
> I am parched with thirst and I perish. Give me quickly
> The cold water flowing forth from the Lake of Memory.

Yet his future was decided differently. There was still sin to atone for, not least the sin of pride, for he seemed never to have learned humility or put his exclusiveness aside. He was pushed to the spring of Lethe, among the smiling and unthinking crowds, to forget and be born again. The water ran blankly down his throat. He was a child of Earth. But before he could return there, the three Fates – the threefold breath that spun, stretched out and neatly severed the thread of his days in the world – summoned him to a place that was murky, cold and running with black water, where he was to choose the new form he would take.

Shivering, he begged the purple-cloaked sisters to be kind to him. But there was little to discuss. He refused, Plato said, to be born again from the body of a woman and take the shape of a man. Women had caused him too much pain. In fact he could not – as he had understood and taught – be incarnated twice in a row in human form. He was bound to take two other shapes before reappearing as a man. Perhaps after three human incarnations only, rather than the ten most men endured, and after three sojourns of a thousand years in the Elysian Fields, he might be worthy of Heaven. Again on the way he would kneel before Persephone, burying his head in her lap in that flickering shrine of wheat and flowers:

I have sunk beneath the bosom of the Mistress, the Queen
    of the Underworld,
And now I come a suppliant to holy Persephone,
That of her grace she may send me to the seats of the
    hallowed.

And Persephone would answer:

Happy and blessed one, thou shalt be god instead of mortal.

He would become 'god from man' then, dissolved into the white, sweet holiness of pure union: in his own, strange, riddling words, 'A kid thou art fallen into milk'.

But that was still far away. The world beckoned again, distant, dark. He was condemned again to 'the wheel'. There was no possibility this time of making human music there. As Tagore understood, Orpheus had sung out his human Fate, and now laid down his silent lyre 'at the feet of the silent':

Ever in my life I sought thee with my songs. It was they who
led me from door to door, and with them have I felt about
me, searching and touching my world.

It was my songs that taught me all the lessons I ever learnt;
they showed me secret paths, they brought before my sight
many a star on the horizon of my heart.

But there were other ways to experience the world, to

make music and to send back praise. At the Earth's edge, therefore – his skin pricking and pluming into pure feathers, his shoulders hunching into huge white wings – he loosened his long, sinuous throat and sang as a swan.

He had watched them as a child. They crowded the banks of the shallow Hebrus and bobbed in the silver river, rising some-times with a harsh, flapping spray of light before subsiding again. Their song, a swooping bugle call, announced the dawn mist clearing; all creation strained to hear it, and the waves on the shore grew still around his small, slipping feet. A simple swan feather, found among the white, scattered stones, showed the filaments of a lyre when he held it against the sun. Swans were sacred to his father Apollo and the willing steeds of Aphrodite, flying where she commanded. They sang most enchantingly only as they drew near death, bowing their necks beneath the grey-green willow trees; but he now carried Death inside him, sharp and sweet, and had made that music, too, his own.

Perhaps it was this swan of light, harnessed by Love, that took wing slowly past Cocteau's tiny apartment in the rue de Monpensier, following the windings of the Seine towards the sea; that walked carefully, on black-webbed feet, across the green lawn by Herbert's study; that sang, with a silver wake, in the lute of Gibbons and the cello of Saint-Saëns; that floated on black water around Sibelius's Tuonela, the island of the dead; or that rose 'in sudden thunder', shocking the young Yeats, from the nine-and-fifty on the lake at Coole:

> That stormy white
> But seems a concentration of the sky;
> And, like the soul, it sails into the sight

Orpheus

And in the morning's gone, no man knows why . . .

Perhaps this was the swan that had waddled years before, clumsily, into Rilke's poems, only to gather speed and run, glide, sail with compelling majesty out across the waters of death. Wave after wave now beat surely, calmly under him, flooding with words. Or else the divine lyre-player in his human shape, sensed in some effect of the lamp or eruption of the stove, installed himself at Rilke's shoulder with just a little pressure, a little breath – that breath that could blow him alive – willing his hand to write, like an eager young man kibitzing at a game of cards.

Or perhaps he came out of innermost silence, as Rilke recorded two weeks later. From his standing-desk that day he noticed 'a feeling' over the laurel, Apollo's tree; a movement in three or four leaves brushed by a butterfly, which then tumbled past his window, 'buoyed by the breath of the valley':

> And now you remember another time,
> when you felt it already so perfect, here,
>
> the silence around a god. But wasn't it *more*?
> Didn't it grow stiller and stiller, progressing
> To stillness, pressing
>
> your pounding heart, which has beaten its way
> into some soundless lull in the afternoon?
> There, He is.

On that extraordinary February morning, Rilke did as he was told. This was 'the most puzzling dictation I have ever received', but he had no choice; inspiration was sweeping

243

ANN WROE

through him 'like a hurricane', a 'divine tempest', cracking and
tearing every fibre as though he was a tree. He paced back and
forth, 'booming' and 'howling' his welcome to these 'unbeliev-
ably vast commands'. Sleep was impossible. Meals were notional.
'God knows what nourished me,' he wrote, although he knew.

Twenty-five sonnets were written in three days, 'in one
breathless act of obedience'. He had expected to finish his
Duino Elegies, and did that too, vying with the angels who had
always overshadowed him, but the utterly unexpected sonnets
kept coming. Each was in perfect metre and rhyme, though
for months beforehand he had abandoned both. They were
like riddles; he did not fully understand them, and thought
they should be printed interleaved with plain paper so that he
could eventually explain them to readers. Where darkness
remained, he told a friend, 'it is the kind that requires not
clarification, but surrender'. He was already sure, however,
that barely a word needed to be changed.

At the end of the first visitation, when the cold white moon
had risen, Rilke ran downstairs to stroke 'like some furry old
animal' the walls of the château that had sheltered Orpheus,
and him. But Orpheus had not gone. This was only a lull, a
Windstille, while he drew in breath between the songs. Between
February 13th and 23rd, thirty-eight more poems appeared.
Rilke wrote them down, shaking, barely able to hold the pen
that recorded the 'still warm' words. He knew now that there
was 'ultimately only one poet, that infinite one, who makes
himself felt here and there through the ages' – and now
possessed him, in the Valais, among the winter trees.

On the morning of February 26th, a Sunday, he went
downstairs to eat with appetite at last. He was aware that after

such a storm there must be a reaction, a fall. But he felt, with Orpheus's life still tingling in him, that he was 'falling into the spring'.

> *Über dem Wandel und Gang,*
> *weiter und freier,*
> *währt noch dein Vor-Gesang,*
> *Gott mit der Leier.*

Beyond the windows, over the hills, fresh clouds were streaming and shape-shifting as fast as the toiling, teeming world. But Orpheus's song rang higher and holier, eternally.

> Suffering we misunderstand,
> Love we have still to learn,
> Death and what lies therein
>
> await unveiling.
> Song alone circles the land,
> hallowing, hailing.

On the table in the empty breakfast room lay – as if magically assembled – his coffee cup, yeasty *Gugelhupf* and a bowl of the first tender primroses brimming with the sun.

Bibliography

Place of publication is London unless otherwise stated.

Translations in this book from ancient authors and from Rilke are taken from several versions and my own. Specific translations are cited in the Bibilography wherever they have been used exclusively.

Ancient sources

Aeschylus *Agamemnon*

Apollodorus. *Library* and *Epitome*, ed. J.G. Frazer

Apollonius Rhodius. *Argonautica*, tr. R.C. Seaton (1912)

Aristophanes: *Plays II: Wasps, Clouds, Birds, Festival Time,* tr. Kenneth McLeish (1993)

Aristotle. *On Music*

Cicero. *The Nature of the Gods*

Diodorus of Sicily. *The Library of History*

Euripides. *Cyclops*; *Hippolytus; The Bacchae,* tr. G.S. Kirk (Cambridge, 1979)

Herodotus. *Histories*

Horace. *Odes; Ars Poetica*

Kern, Otto. *Orphicorum fragmenta* (Berlin, 1922)

Orpheus, attr. *Argonautica*, tr. and ed. Francis Vian, Collection des
universités de France, Belles Lettres (Paris, 2003)

——*Argonautica Hymni; Libellus de Lapidibus [Lithica] et Fragmenta*, cum
notis H. Stephani et Andr. Christ. Eschenbachii (Leipzig, 1764)

——Anon. *The Book of the Orphic Hymns, together with the principal
fragments of other hymns attributed to Orpheus*, printed in uncial
letters as a typographical experiment (1827); see also Taylor,
Thomas; Athanassakis, Apostolos

Ovid. *Metamorphoses*, tr. Mary M. Innes (1955)

Pausanias. *Description of Greece*

Pindar. *Pythian Odes* 4

Philostratus. Flavius, *Life of Apollonius*

Philostratus the Elder and Younger. *Imagines*, tr. Arthur Fairbanks
(1931)

Plato. *Critias*; *Laws*; *Philebus*; *Symposium*; *Timaeus*

Plutarch. *Moralia*, Book 9

Seneca. *Hercules Furens; Hercules Oetaeus; Medea*. Tr. Frank Justus
Miller (1917)

Virgil. *Aeneid*, Book 6; *Eclogues*, Book 3; *Georgics*, Books 3 and 4,
tr. C. Day Lewis, (Oxford, 1940)

Early Christian, medieval and early modern sources

Anon, *Sir Orfeo*, ed. A.J. Bliss (Oxford, 1954)

Bacon, Francis, *Of the Wisdom of the Ancients* (1609)

Boethius. *The Consolation of Philosophy*, tr. V.E. Watts (1998)

Calderón de la Barca. *El divino Orfeo*

Clement of Alexandria. *Writings*, Ante-Nicene Christian Library,
Vol. 4 (2 vols, Edinburgh, 1867)

Gluck, C.W. von. *Orfeo*, compiled by Patricia Howard (Cambridge,
1981)

Henryson, Robert. *Orpheus and Eurydice*, in *The Poems of Robert Henryson*, ed. Denton Fox (Oxford, 1981)

Iamblichus. *On the Mysteries of the Egyptians, Chaldeans & Assyrians*, tr. Thomas Taylor (1821; 3rd edition, 1968)

——*On the Pythagorean Life*, tr. with notes by Gillian Clark (Liverpool, 1989)

Marsilio Ficino. *Letters*, tr. by members of the Language Department of the School of Economic Science, London, 10 vols (1975)

Milton, John. *Poetical Works*

Monteverdi, Claudio. *Orfeo*, ed. John Whenham, Cambridge Opera Handbooks (Cambridge, 1986)

Poliziano, Angelo. *A translation of the* Orpheus *of Angelo Politan and the* Aminta *of Torquato Tasso*, with an introductory essay on the pastoral by Louis E. Lord (1931)

Proclus. *Commentaries on Plato's* Parmenides, tr. Glenn R. Morrow and John M. Dillon (Princeton, 1987)

——*Commentaries on Plato's* Timaeus, Vol. 2, Book 2: *Proclus on the Causes of the Cosmos and its Creation*, tr. and ed. David T. Runia and Michael Share (Cambridge, 2008)

Rumi, Mevlana Jalaluddin. *The Collection: An Anthology of Translations*, ed. Kabir Helminski (Boston, 2005)

——*Mystical poems of Rumi, first selection, poems 1-200*, tr. A.J. Arberry (Chicago, 1968)

Sidney, Sir Philip. *A Defence of Poesy* (1595)

Taylor, Thomas, tr. *The Mystical Initiations; or, Hymns of Orpheus*. First edition (1787); second edition (Chiswick, 1824)

——tr. *The Cratylus, Phaedo, Parmenides, Timaeus and Critias of Plato* (reprinted Minneapolis, 1976)

Theophilus of Antioch. *Ad Autolycum*, tr. Robert M. Grant (Oxford, 1970)

Modern sources

Apollinaire, Guillaume. *Le Bestiaire ou cortège d'Orphée* (Paris, 1911)

Anouilh, Jean. *Eurydice* (1942)

Archibald, Z.H. *The Odryssian Kingdom of Thrace: Orpheus Unmasked* (Oxford 1998)

Athanassakis, Apostolos N. *The Orphic Hymns* (Missoula, 1977)

Axon, William E.A. 'Thomas Taylor, the Platonist', reprinted from *The Library*, August 1890 (www.archive.org)

Bacon, J.R. 'The Geography of the Orphic *Argonautica*' *Classical Quarterly*, Vol. 25. No. 3–4 (July-Oct 1931), pp. 172–183

Beazley, J.D. *Attic Red-figure Vase-Painters* (Oxford, 1963)

Bernstock, Judith E., *Under the Spell of Orpheus: The Persistence of a Myth in Twentieth-Century Art* (Carbondale, 1991)

Betegh, Gábor. *The Derveni Papyrus: Cosmology, Theology and Interpretation* (Cambridge, 2004)

Brown, Bruce Alan. *Gluck and the French Theatre in Vienna* (1991)

Bruns, Gerald L. *Maurice Blanchot:The Refusal of Philosophy* (Baltimore, 1997)

Burkert, Walter. *Greek Religion, Archaic and Classical*, tr. John Raffan (Oxford, 1985)

Butler, E.M. *Rainer Maria Rilke* (Cambridge, 1941)

Cocteau, Jean. *The Art of Cinema*, comp. and ed. André Bernard and Claude Gauteur; tr. Robin Buss (1992)

——*Orphée: Tragédie en un acte et un entr'acte* (1933)

——*Orphée: The Play and the Film*, ed. Edward Freeman (Bristol, 1992)

Cosmopoulos, Michael B. *Greek Mysteries:The Archaeology and Ritual of Ancient Greek Secret Cults* (2003)

Dimitrokalis, Georges. 'La Tete Coupée d'Orphée: Re-examination et Ré-interpretation d'un Mythe Ancien', www.myriobilos.gr/texts/french/dimitrokalis_orphee.html

Downing, Christine. 'Looking back at Orpheus', *Spring 71: Orpheus*, Fall 2004 (New Orleans, 2004)

Duffy, Carol Ann. *The World's Wife* (1999)

Eisler, Robert. *Orpheus – The Fisher: Comparative Studies in Orphic and Early Christian Cult Symbolism* (1921)

Ferguson, Kitty. *Pythagoras: His Lives and the Legacy of a Rational Universe* (New York, 2008)

Francis, Lesley Lee. 'Edward Thomas: "The Lyre" and "The Bouquet"', *Edward Thomas Fellowship Newsletter* 40 (January 1999), p. 14

Frazer, J.G. *The Golden Bough: A Study in Magic and Religion*. 3rd edition (1963)

Freden, Gustaf. *Orpheus and the Goddess of Nature*, Acta Universitatis Gothoburgensis, Vol. 64 (Gothenburg, 1958)

Friedman, John Block. *Orpheus in the Middle Ages* (Cambridge, Mass. 1970)

Gaiman, Neil, and others. *Sandman Special # 1: The Song of Orpheus* (DC Comics, New York, November 1991)

Graves, Robert. *The White Goddess* (1948)

Gros Louis, Kenneth R.R. 'The Triumph and Death of Orpheus in the English Renaissance'. *Studies in English Literature, 1500–1900*, Vol. 9, No. 1, *The English Renaissance* (Winter, 1969), pp. 63–80 (Rice University, 1969)

Guthrie, W.K.C. *Orpheus and Greek Religion: A Study of the Orphic Movement* (1935)

Hamburger, Michael. *Reason and Energy: Studies in German Literature* (1957)

Harvey, Andrew. *The Way of Passion: A Celebration of Rumi* (Berkeley, 1994). (For translations on pp. 41, 193)

Howard, Patricia. *Gluck: an eighteenth-century portrait in letters and documents* (Oxford, 1995)

Jesnick, Ilona Julia. *The Image of Orpheus in Roman Mosaic* (BAR International Series 671, 1997)

Jung, Carl. *Memories, Dreams, Reflections*, recorded and ed. Aniela Jaffé (1963)

——*The Red Book* = *Liber novus*, ed. Sonu Shamdasani, tr. Mark Kyburz, John Peck and Sonu Shamdasani (New York, 2009)

Lee, Owen M., 'Mystic Orpheus: Another note on the three-figure reliefs'. *Hesperia*, Vol. 33, No. 4 (Oct-Dec 1964), pp. 401–4

Mead, G.R.S. *Orpheus* (1896; John Watkins reprint, 1965); www.theosophical.ca/orpheusPIGRSM.html

Milosz, Czeslaw. *Second Space: New Poems*, tr. the author and Robert Hass (New York, 2005)

Nietzsche, Friedrich. *The Birth of Tragedy, or Hellenism and Pessimism*, tr. William A. Haussmann (1910).

O'Donaghue, David. 'Orpheus and the Birth of non-representational Art'. *Spring 71: Orpheus*. Fall 2004 (New Orleans, 2004)

Paget, R.F., *In the Footsteps of Orpheus: The story of the finding and identification of the lost entrance to Hades* (1967)

Prater, Donald, *A Ringing Glass: The Life of Rainer Maria Rilke* (Oxford, 1986)

Rilke, Rainer Maria. *Ahead of All Parting: Poetry and Prose of Rainer Maria Rilke*, tr. Stephen Mitchell (New York, 1995)

——*Duino Elegies*, tr. J.B. Leishmann and Stephen Spender (1939, rev. ed. 1948, 1963). (For translation p. 170)

——*Duino Elegies and Sonnets to Orpheus*, ed. and tr. Stephen Mitchell (New York, 1982). (For translations on pp. 65, 83, 206, 236)

——*Letters to Merline*, tr. Jesse Browner (1990)

——*Letters to a Young Poet*, tr. Stephen Cohn (2000)

——*Neue Gedichte/New Poems (1907–8): The German text, with a translation, introduction and notes,* by J.B. Leishman (1964)

——*Rainer Maria Rilke and Lou Andreas-Salomé: The Correspondence,* tr. Edward Snow and Michael Winkler (2006)

——*Rilke: Selected Poems,* tr. Ruth Spiers (1942). For 'Orpheus, Eurydice, Hermes': see pp. 124, 162–3, 172

——*Selected Letters of Rainer Maria Rilke,* tr. R.F.C.Hull (1946)

——*Sonnets to Orpheus,* tr. Stephen Cohn (2000). (For translations on pp. 20, 107, 109, 112, 184, 227, 235)

Romanyshyn, Robert. 'The Orphic Roots of Jung's Psychology', *Spring 71, Orpheus,* Fall 2004 (New Orleans, 2004)

Segal, Charles. *Orpheus: The Myth of the Poet* (Baltimore, 1989)

Spate, Virginia. *Orphism: The evolution of non-figurative painting in Paris 1910–1914* (Oxford, 1979)

Stevens, Wallace. *Selected Poems* (1953)

Tagore, Rabindranath. *Gitanjali,* tr. by the author, with an introduction by W.B. Yeats (1913)

Thomas, Edward. *Collected Poems* (2004)

Warden, John, ed., *Orpheus: The Metamorphoses of a Myth* (Toronto, 1982)

West, M. L. *Ancient Greek Music* (Oxford, 1992)

——'Odyssey and Argonautica'. *Classical Quarterly,* New Series Vol. 55 (2005), pp. 39–64

——*The Orphic Poems* (Oxford, 1983)

Williams, James S., *Jean Cocteau* (Manchester, 2006)

Yeats, W. B. Collected Poems (for 'Coole and Ballylee, 1913')

Acknowledgements

My thanks especially to Nushi Asenova and Ivor, our driver, who guided me through Bulgaria; to Professor Nicholas Roe of St Andrews University, who changed my mind at a crucial point in the project; to Professor M.L. West for musical advice (any mistakes that remain are my own!); to Nomi Rowe for her encouragement; to my eldest son Simon, for introducing me to Rilke's poetry in the beginning; and to Dan Franklin and Tom Avery at Jonathan Cape, for enthusiasm, kindness and hard work, as ever. Lastly, to Malcolm, my thanks for his constant support and love.

A. W.

Index

255